MW01110019

Women Win
Against All ODDS!

JESUS, COFFEE, & PRAYER
Christian Publishing House

Presented by:
The Q.U.E.E.N Xperience CEO & Founder
Min. Nakita Davis
~A Queen Collaborative~

Copyright © 2020 Min. Nakita Davis
Women Win: Against All ODDS!/ All rights reserved.
No part of this publication may be reproduced, distributed, or transmitted in any
form or by any means, including photocopying, recording, or other electronic or
mechanical methods, without the prior written permission of the publisher, except in
the case of brief quotations embodied in critical reviews and certain other
noncommercial uses permitted by copyright law. For permission requests, write to
the publisher, addressed "Attention: Permissions Coordinator," at the address below.

info@jesuscoffeeandprayer.com – Publishing House

Scriptures marked NIV are taken from the NEW INTERNATIONAL
VERSION (NIV): Scripture taken from THE HOLY BIBLE, NEW
INTERNATIONAL VERSION ®. Copyright© 1973, 1978, 1984, 2011 by
Biblica, Inc.™. Used by permission of Zondervan Scriptures marked NKJV are
taken from the NEW KING JAMES VERSION (NKJV): Scripture taken from
the NEW KING JAMES VERSION®. Copyright© 1982 by Thomas Nelson,
Inc. Used by permission.
Scripture quotations taken from the
New American Standard Bible:registered: (NASB),
Copyright :copyright: 1960, 1962, 1963, 1968, 1971, 1972, 1973,
1975, 1977, 1995 by The Lockman Foundation
Used by permission. www.Lockman.org"
Scripture quotations marked (NLT) are taken from the Holy Bible, New Living
Translation, copyright :copyright:1996, 2004, 2015 by Tyndale House
Foundation. Used by permission of Tyndale House Publishers, a Division of
Tyndale House Ministries, Carol Stream, Illinois 60188. All rights reserved.

All rights reserved ISBN: 978-1-952273-08-7

Cover: RebecaCovers
Layout/Design: Oprahgraphic
Editor: McBright
Publisher:

Jesus, Coffee, and Prayer Christian Publishing House LLC.
1700 Northside Drive, Suite A7, Unit #4-5055 Atlanta, GA 30318
www.jesuscoffeeandprayer.com

Join Our Next Best-Selling Anthology?
Publish Your Own Best-Selling Book?

Women Win Against All ODDS!

Become our Next Elite Influential Women Who Win Honoree?
Visit www.jesuscoffeeandprayer.com
to Book Your Best-Selling Book Consultation or

Email us:
Info@jesuscoffeeandprayer.com

Follow us to stay inspired and encouraged to run your race
FB https://www.facebook.com/jesuscoffeeandprayer
IG https://www.instagram.com/jesuscoffeeandprayer

B,
I pray you are inspired by this read and may you continue to be blessed.
Best Wishes,
Senator Gatra
#VOIRBELLE

B,
You are my inspiration honey. From your styling skills to your accessories you are the best.
Miesha

Table of Contents

A Note From The Publisher Of Purpose

@Jesuscoffeeandprayer

Queen,

this book was designed to specifically encourage you in this season of uncertainty. Many times, we can remain confident when we know the perceived outcome…. When the waters are calm and there is no sight of a storm.

Queen, that is the easy part.

The real challenge, the real testament of your Faith, your perseverance, and the strength that lies within you, can ONLY truly be seen during times of adversity.

Times such as these.

When Covid-19 hit our world~ Every single soul was impacted.

It was inevitable and there was no way around it.

But Thanks be to God, the Queens listed within these chapters are STILL Determined to walk in their land of milk and honey!

I AM TOO AND SO CAN YOU!

By Faith and Jesus Christ as my foundation, I speak healing, restoration, abundance, rejuvenation, and overflow in Every Dry area of Your Life!

Queen, You are a Winner.... NEVER Let anyone tell you different, or anything sway your mind.

We all fall down at some point in our life; but the question is how many times you *Choose* to Get Back Up!

In this season, I am Calling You to Play Your Royal Position and GET UP!

2020 is NOT CANCELLED and neither is any other year thereafter. If you are still breathing and still have warm blood flowing through your veins, then you have an opportunity that many can no longer see.

In this season it is time to be Grateful and innovative with the gifts, the tools and resources you do have; Trust God on an even GREATER level, and tap into the Power of Collaboration.

Women Win Against All ODDS!

When Women link up in Faith, in Collaboration, and Not Competition, the World Takes Notice.

This is how Women Win: Against All Odds!

My Prayer for You

Heavenly Father,

Thank You for being gracious, loving, merciful, and supplying all our needs in this season.

Many have fallen during this time; but you saw fit for each Queen who is reading this page to be here~ to remain~ & to Grow!

I ask right now, that you remove all that hinders. Remove any self-limiting doubts and any negativity that would keep your daughters stagnant and stuck. I pray for your wisdom and discernment to be poured out on your children, sons and daughters in this season.

I pray for hearts that will find their way back to you, repent, and flee from the sin that entangles.

May each reader be blessed richly as you desire, some 10, some 30, some 60 fold.

In Jesus Name I Pray

Amen!

Dedication

In Loving Memory of Regina Cruz

Women Win Queen Coauthor:

Rhonda Anita's Mother

The Process

Rhonda Anita

"Be not afraid of their faces: for I am with thee to deliver thee, saith the LORD."
- Jeremiah 1:8 (KJV)

How do YOU WIN? Especially in a world of two pandemics, racial injustice and COVID-19, winning can seem so far off. Oh, but darling, I beg to differ. Your winning season is right at your doorstep. Right when you want to give up, the ram in the bush becomes the bush. God has been faithful to me, and He has never been a respecter of person. I am Minister Rhonda Anita, author, international best seller, certified life coach with the focus on healing. Being a transformational speaker, CEO and founder of Amazing Life Empowerment Group and Rose of Sharon, a domestic violence organization, recently awarded with the Congressman John Lewis Ambassador Award are among a few of my ultra-dynamic accomplishments.

But you know what, in all that glory, life wasn't always like that for me. There were many times when I didn't know who I was. I relied on the world to teach me who I was and how I should feel. I was a chameleon for many years. I would easily become who you thought I should be just to fit in. See, I am an overcomer of child abuse, domestic violence, three suicide attempts, and I sold my body for a living. I share all these stories in my first book, *Don't Spill the Tea*.

All of these traumatic experiences happened at a very early age. My foundation was highly discombobulated causing me to carry a lot of pain. I tried anything I could to mask the hurt. Thankfully I gave my life to Christ at a young age, around twenty-two to twenty-four years of age. Prior to that, I never thought I would win at anything. As a matter of fact, I recall thinking "I would be lucky to live past the age of twenty-five." How crazier can it get?

I was lost, confused, and without any hope. By the time I became Christ-like, all of the beautiful well-put-together-Christian women looked different to me. When they shared their testimonies, I didn't hear a voice like mine. I heard things that many of us face today, which are totally fine. However, no one around me had a disgusting story as mine, of being broken and abused; how about being the very fantasy that their husbands caused harm to their wives for. No one was like me. How could I stand up and share what God saved me from in the face of these perfect women? So, I put on a mask for many years trying to be the very image that without my story, I could appear to be for others.

Then I read the scripture, Jeremiah 1:8: *"Be not afraid of their faces: for I am with thee to deliver thee, saith the LORD."* This scripture helped me to see that man is mere flesh. God delivered me from so many things, and I need to share that with the world. Right now, I cancel out shame and declare that you are the righteousness of God. I casted out fear and proclaim that you walk in total peace. I denounce confusion and release clarity over your life in the name of Jesus! I just felt that right there for someone, hallelujah! Because so many of us deal with some unspoken truths and pain in silence.

I created an event called *Living Behind the Mask*. It's a high caliber masquerade-gala that honors those that suffer in silence due to domestic violence. When I reflected on simply finding my voice was when I grew in courage, boldness, and pride of my story. God created me a winner and a champion. Just like He did for me He has taken your pain and made it your purpose: from a mess to giving you a message. God took me from making $8.00 an hour with only a GED to a college graduate and full-time business owner. Among empowering women to find their own voice through healing and forgiveness, I am also a real estate leading lady and a CEO of a Nonprofit organization that help to heal women from domestic violence and sex trafficking.

Through God, I have reinvented myself on so many occasions. With some things I learned along the way, I am going to share three points of process for success that I like you to ponder while walking into your winning season.

Process One:

According to Romans 5:3-5 (NLT):

> *We can rejoice, too, when we run into problems and trials, for we know that they help us develop endurance. And endurance develops strength of character, and character strengthens our confident hope of salvation. And this hope will not lead to disappointment. For we know how dearly*

God loves us, because he has given us the Holy Spirit to fill our hearts with his love.

Never give up when you have been knocked down. Understand that a tree grows down first before it grows up. Trials and tribulation come to sharpen your tools. The anointing is increased by the tears and lessons you learn. I have been divorced twice, yet I am still hopeful that true love exists for me. I know myself better, and I am much more equipped to be the wife my husband needs. I am destined for greatness and all that God has me on this earth to accomplish, and with every breath I have in me, I am going to do it. Recalibrate, reinvent, revise, and remember your *why*.... The word *remember* means to practice over and over, again. Remember your why. If it is not big enough you will give up every time. It is time to find out your why and go get it!

Process Two:

God is always the focus of my love, my life, my foundation, my family, my empire, and my legacy. Exodus 20:3 (NIV) says, **"You shall have no other gods before me."** The Father is my compass for everything in my world. God is bigger than anything you will ever come in contact with. Make God bigger in your life because without Him nothing is possible anyway, but with Him all things are possible to him that believes (Mark 9:23).

Despite all of this planning, I truly believe that you cannot get new wine in old wine skin. Let me simplify this a little. Would you agree that when your face is clean past the surface level, then make-up will lay flawlessly? Have you ever had a facial? It is a painful purging process but offers many benefits. It reduces stress, cleanses your skin, prevents aging, promotes blood circulation, rejuvenates your skin, detoxifies the skin and treats acne, to name a few. For me, I am

4

one of those who scab over after a facial, that doesn't seem that pleasant huh? Interestingly enough, just like an oil change in your car, your skin needs to be purified to function at its optimal level. Did you know that skin is an organ? As a matter of fact, it is the largest organ on your body, yet we invest in everything else but skin care.

I can testify that when going through the purging process there is some discomfort, just like a facial. When the esthetician is digging, squeezing and pulling your skin and extracting all those impurities, it can be quite painful. It doesn't matter how good it smells in the room; it doesn't matter how comfortable the bed is that you are laying on, you have to go through the process to reveal new skin. Then, you can enjoy the rejuvenation process that reveals the skin that has been wanting to be shown off.

Well, it is similar to purging those impurities from your heart space. I think that as life dishes us blow after blow, we find ourselves rebounding, and not because we learned from the pain or better off after the pain. I have witnessed that many of our resilience come from a deep-down desire to thrive in the face of adversity. I get that! The problem with this is we never heal, instead we develop calluses around our heart, and when disappointment arises again, we are stone cold and do everything we can to ensure that we don't feel the pain of the past. In my international best-selling book *The Rebirth*, I teach on ways to finding your happiness again by taking time to notice "Hey, I just went through something, I am hurt." This is because once you acknowledge you're hurt, you have created a plan of forgiveness and healing. Healing and forgiveness don't happen by osmosis. After all I have been through, I am a firm believer that in Him I live, move and have my being. Nonetheless, time doesn't heal all wounds. It is a deliberate focus on healing that heals all wounds. Make God large in your life and allow the Holy Spirit to purge everything in your heart that is not like Him. Psalm 51:10 (NIV) proclaims, *"Create in me a pure heart, O God, and renew a steadfast spirit within me."*

The moments you clean your closet for spring or change out your smoke detector batteries can be used as a simple reminder to take a moment and check your heart and see if there is anything you are holding onto that is blocking you from manifesting your dream in this winning season. Psalm 139:23-24: *"Search me, God, and know my heart; test me and know my anxious thoughts. See if there is any offensive way in me, and lead me in the way everlasting."*

Process Three:

Finally, this last process is going to go against everything that you have been taught about work, life, and balancing. Finding a balance is what many try so hard to accomplish in order to achieve their zenith level. Consider this: finding a balance is an illusion, instead finding our flow, the flow of your own meditation and manifestation is truly living the American Dream. As a mother, entrepreneur, creative person, wife, minister, friend, or servant, etc., I can honestly say I don't practice balance. I find myself in the flow of life as I see what's best for me. The way I see it, is as if I am a clock where I am the center of the wheel and God is the wheel.

The hands on the clock never stop. There are times when the flow is in seconds, minutes and hours. Therefore, time is never balanced. Time is always flowing, but flowing forward. On any given workday, we know that there are regular business hours, yet we somehow seem to find time to talk to our spouses, go to lunch with a friend, and still plan for our family vacation. This is proof that we are completely capable of following the flow that our blessed lives provide for us. I normally look at my calendar and budget, before I say *yes* to anybody for any occasion. I live by my calendar. I am typically never late; I am often proactive. However, if I lose sight of an appointment, bill or important obligation, then I know I am out of my alignment, and something that I took on was not a God-given assignment. Everything is not for everyone at every moment. Instead, take some time at the top of the year and write down the visions for yourself in these following areas: business, health, family, friends, God and finances.

Habakkuk 2:2: *"Then the LORD said to me, 'Write my answer plainly on tablets, so that a runner can carry the correct message to others.'"* When we fail to plan, we plan to fail. When you are able to write the visions and how much time and where you will put your money in these areas, then when other things arise that don't fit your budget/vision, you can decide if they will fit into your time and money flow. These are only a few areas. You may have more such as self-care. You must allocate time for yourself as well. What does that look like for you? Now I am totally aware that you won't be able to predict everything. However, when opportunities come knocking on your door your will be able to clearly define where that opportunity will fit in your life, what category, and will it take you away too much from one area over another. Everything is connected in total alignment, not balance. One definition of balance says it's "a condition in which different elements are equal or in the correct proportions." I just don't believe that I can give equal portions of myself to different many things. The ratios look something like this 10:20:30:5:35, and that is not balance at all. We all have the same twenty-four hours a day, and based on priority, it is my recommendation to breakdown your day into percentages that will equally yield the results that you deem to be successful for that day.

During the pandemics I found a new voice, a louder voice, a stronger flow. I realized that time was up and that the difference I can make

Nicole Richardson helps powerful women win rich with the Nikki Rich Show, bringing awareness to her battle end-stage Renal Disease (kidney disease) by telling her story and sharing her faith as a Christian.

Women Win Rich with the Nikki Rich Show,

In 2011, Nicole Richardson created *The Nikki Rich Show* in Charlotte, NC. Fast forward to years later, while living in Los Angeles, California, Nicole has grown her network to over 2.2 million in combined audience. With this growth, *Women Win with The Nikki Rich Show* became a source for entertainment, live-streaming interviews, music, utilizing media marketing tools and promotional strategies in helping build brands through social media.

Women win through the success of the *Nikki Rich Show* as the show provides entertainment by celebrating women's talents. Women win rich by getting updates on new content, performing their music live, and sharing their videos to millions of people, thus increasing their networks and revenue. The *Nikki Rich Show* live-stream interviews are key promoting brands providing a diversity of views we deal with day to day.

Women Win Rich by bringing awareness to the journey of Kidney disease.

Everyone has a story. Nicole helps women win rich by bringing awareness to kidney disease. In Sept 2017, she was diagnosed with end-stage renal disease (kidney failure). At the time, she was heartbroken, discouraged and didn't know what to do. From the day she found out, she knew that she had to step up. Nicole Richardson began educating herself and others on the disease, the process and ways to cope with the disease.

How do women win rich?

"God is in the midst of her; she shall not be moved; God will help her when morning dawns" (Psalm 46:5 ESV).

Many young women have kidney disease but do not like to talk about it. Nicole shares that having a daily journal will have women winning. Daily journaling and having notes help to keep memories alive, as you learn, grow and develop. Women Win Rich journaling helps to express your thoughts and feelings. Daily journals help women to win rich and make positive changes in life. Writing journal motivates and encourages while on a growth journey.

Women Win Rich sharing faith and belief in God

Nicole is always open about her faith and belief in God. She shares her life experiences to help other women in faith. There are many times when we all feel like we have no one to talk too, but we do. As a Christian, let it go and give it to God. When first moving to California, Nicole stepped out in faith; she knew in her heart where she was supposed to be, through constant prayer.

Throughout life, we all want to win! Whatever happens, women win rich in *Nikki Rich Show* by bringing awareness to battle end-stage renal disease (kidney disease) and sharing faith. One verse that stands out to Nicole is Matthew 6:33: "But seek first the kingdom of God and his righteousness, and all these things will be added to you."

About the Author:

Nicole Richardson known as "Nikki Rich" is originally from a small town of Seneca, South Carolina and currently living in Los Angeles. She is a television and radio personality of the *Nikki Rich Show*, media influencer, Oprah Winfrey Network Ambassador, media & press, and #1 Amazon best-selling published author and speaker.

Nicole's accomplishments and hard work had led her where she is today, having started broadcasting since the age of nine. She was a former seven-year educator of the Charlotte Mecklenburg County School System. She is in her second year of Doctoral in Business Administration, MBA, from University of Phoenix, with Bachelor of Science in Criminal Justice, Education minor from USC Spartanburg known as USC Upstate.

Nicole Richardson, one of social media's influential black business woman and entrepreneurs demographics' are 2.3 Million impressions and thirty-four thousand followers on Instagram. Nicole's engaging audience demographics include fifty-eight (58%) and forty-two percent (42%) for male and female respectively, and with interaction in the top cities of Los Angeles, New York, Houston, Atlanta and Charlotte.

Currently, Nicole Richardson has recently had the pleasure of being an Oprah Winfrey Network Ambassador/ Media, interviewing at the OWN offices the cast of the different shows. Nicole was in the media & Press for *Oprah's Life you want* tour in San Jose, California. In Jan. 2018, Nicole was personally invited to celebrate with Oprah, her birthday at OWN.

Nicole Richardson has recently gained worldwide stardom with her talk show by interviewing celebrities, entrepreneurs, tech companies and sports athletes. She has interviewed on the red carpets of top awards Shows as follows: the Academy Awards (Oscars), Nab-Show in Las Vegas, Tech Emmys in Las Vegas and Creative Arts Emmys in Los Angeles, MTVu Woodie Award in Austin, BET Hip Hop Awards in Miami, BET Experience In Los Angeles, Soul Train Awards & Stellar Awards in Las Vegas and the NAACP Image awards in Los Angeles, California.

Nicole Richardson Celebrity has had Interviews and interactions with Oprah, Tyler Perry, Richard & Kathy Hilton, Ava Durvernay, Conan O' Brian, David Spade, Diddy, Snoop Dogg, Comcast, Adobe, IBM, Sprockett, youtube founders- Steven Chen & Chad Hurly, Adam sharp President Of NATAS, David Pogue-CBS Yahoo, Gloria Allred, Tina knowles Lawson-Beyonce's mother & designer, Cardi B, Iggy Azalea, DapperDan of Harlem, Matt Barnes, Chris Rock, New Edition, Bobby Brown, Judges -Alex, Faith, Lauren Lake, and Mablean, Joe & Jermaine Jackson and so many more.

Nicole Richardson's is also a #1 Amazon international best-selling author for the book *Breast Easy*. She speaks across the nation at tech panels, and empowers thousands at universities. She advocates kidney disease awareness, having been diagnosed of same two years ago, in non-profit organizations, volunteering her time and media team.

As a media influencer whose talents and unprecedented hustle as a host, writer, producer, and educator are unmatched, she is known for the Toyota RAV 4 series featured host, contributor, and have been seen making appearances on TMZ Live, Fox 11 in Los Angeles, Fox 5 in Philly, Bill Cunningham Show on The CW on K-Cal , Comcast & Spectrum ch32, AT&At Uverse.

CONNECT WITH NICOLE RICHARDSON "NIKKI RICH"

Website: TheNikkiRichShow.com
Instagram: @MsNikkiRich @NikkiRichShowtv
Twitter: @MsNikkiRich @NikkiRichShowtv
Facebook: @NikkiRichShowtv
Youtube: NikkiRich2

Destined to Win...It's in our D.N.A.

Franchesca Ross-Jones

"Now faith is the assurance of things hoped for,
the conviction of things not seen."
- Hebrews 11:1 (NIV)

"For my thoughts are not your thoughts,
neither are your ways my ways, saith the LORD."
- Isaiah 55:8 (NIV)

As women, we are destined to win. I know you may be saying to yourself, "Really, I can't tell" or "What do you know about me?" Beloved, you are no different than I am neither am I any different than you are. We are optimistic, driven, persistent, accountable, courageous, grateful, loving, nurturing, strong, and God-fearing change agents. We are all women: mothers, grandmothers, wives, daughters, sisters, cousins, aunts, entrepreneurs, corporate career masterminds, co-workers, church members, best friends, friends, mentors, and the lists go on. We have been, or may still yet become each of those women at some point in our lives.

I've been a teenage mother, single mother, and single woman; I had lost my job, had more bills every month than the paycheck, had multiple jobs and still couldn't make ends meet, had my heart broken a few times, my car repossessed, my first home foreclosed on, lost my corporate job without notice, mistreated by those I love most, talked about, lied on, and experienced church hurt, you name? I've been there too. Yes, it hurts. I am not saying it will not come or that it does not hurt because life comes with its solutions as well as its challenges.

Life can bring immeasurable sunshine and sometimes, what may feel as though infinite pain. Just being candid, each of us has a plan for our lives. We have a vision of what we feel our lives should look like. When that plan deviates – failed business, job displaced, forced career change, challenges with our kids, downturns in our health, loss of a loved one, divorce, etc. What is next? How do you go on when life as you know it has just been snatched right from under you? How do you weather yet another storm of life? Oh! Queen, stand in faith and keep believing! Rain is good for us. It is refreshing. It is cleansing. It opens a door and an opportunity to let some things go so that we are prepared to receive and embrace what is to come.

God doesn't give you the people you want, He gives you the people you *need*, to help you, to hurt you, to leave you, to love you and to make you into the person you were meant to be. Sometimes, it takes someone else's perspective; the perspective of an empowered woman to remind you of your strength and reassure you that it is okay to let go and move forward into unchartered territory. You may be discouraged, but know that God will not fail you. God is with us through all our pains, hurts, uncertainties, disappointments, and struggles. I look in the mirror every morning, and I tell myself, no matter what it looks like I will continue to walk by faith and not by sight. My queen, you must continue to keep the faith, until the manifestation of God is done. I know it can be hard to stay faithful when what you can see and feel in the natural seems hopeless.

The blessing, lesson, or experience that shaped my strongest perspective on women being destined to win was when I became a mother at the tender age of sixteen years. That life change immediately prompted me to grow up fast. I had to decide to either become the woman that God called me to become or to become the woman that the world said I would become. I have been ungracefully broken in my lifetime, but I thank my God for I eventually became gracefully broken. I thank God for His grace in Isaiah 55:8 where He says, "For my thoughts are not your thoughts, neither are your ways my ways, saith the LORD." God can use times of unexpected changes in our lives for good. And His best is always worth the wait. It is something about God's Grace and Mercy, Beloved. His process produces passion and purpose and I have to tell you, it is a beautiful thing.

When I became a mother, I began to rethink my priorities and my life. There was an immediate shift from being a care-free teenager to an intentional mommy. I decided to become intentional about my actions, priorities, life, and my baby's life. God granted me an opportunity for realignment at such a young age. I positively embraced the life change and discovered that the value of certain things had significantly changed for me. Not only had I become a new mother, I saw my own mother in the fight of her life. As I began life as a mom, my mom's health began to deteriorate. She was diagnosed with an aggressive neuropathy that affected her mobility and ease of her daily living. Life has taught me to have that "now faith" as seen in Hebrews 11:1 where it reminds us of faith in action saying that "Now faith is the assurance of things hoped for, the conviction of things not seen." I began to appreciate the brokenness

I was experiencing. Through the tears and the fear, I gained a deeper dependence on God. He had always been the driving force in my life. Life has a way of applying pressure that is not always easy to relieve.

Do you ever find yourself setting goals, and if by chance you don't accomplish what you set out to, you feel like it is the end of the world? I have and sometimes, I still do. The blessing over the years is that I have learned that when I surrender to God, the feelings of stress and anxiety seem to fade away. I know that may sound crazy to you. Honestly, when I look back on it, it seems more of easier said than done. I can recall finding myself in my twenties broken in personal and professional relationships, broken in my finances, career, and in so many areas of life. I remember feeling as if everything I was dealing with came without any warning and pretty much, caught me by surprise. Every time I thought I was turning a corner and on the brink of my *greater*, there always seemed to be a detour. I think because I have always been determined and driven, God would not allow distractions to keep my attention for too long. The amazing power of God is that He already knows our paths. God knows infinite time. He knows what will happen in our lives and when. I have always been focused on what I wanted to do, where I wanted to go, and where I wanted to end up. God allowed every disappointment, detour, mistake, and every single part of my story – good and not so good. Queens! Straighten your crown, in all your ways acknowledge Him and He will direct your path. Hold onto God's unchanging hand and most importantly, continue to trust God, even when you cannot trace Him. Let me let you in on a little secret: if you want to be somebody, somebody special, just be you.

Oftentimes, I remember walking in darkness and confusion. However, self-reflection has been a major thing for me. My faith has been a major thing for me. My relationship with God is especially important to me. My love for God has been a major thing in forming me into the woman I am today. I strive to be the *Proverbs 31 woman* all the time, and I am in training daily. Thankfully, God always knows the way forward, even when we do not know where to begin. The plans He has for me have helped me evolve into the God-fearing woman I am, the entrepreneur, the friend, the daughter, the sister, the wife and the mother. I strive daily to be that mother, that wife, that friend, that woman who I have been called to be. I take all the rain and I let it wash away what needs to be cleansed so that I can make room for what is to come.

Do not be afraid of what is around the corner, rather embrace it. Empowered women empower other women. We are not petty. We are intellectually challenging, honest, genuine, ambitious, consistent, classy and empathetic. Keep walking forward. Keep moving forward. It is okay to be in the valley, but not to get there and get stuck and stay there. Learn the lesson and execute it. Keep pushing. You are going places, Beloved, places you never dreamed, and places you never imagined. From this moment on, grow in God's promises for your life, for they are real! Remember that we are women who win. It is in our D.N.A. I love you.

About the Author:

A God-fearing woman, and a woman on a mission, Franchesca Ross-Jones faced hardships and financial struggles as a single mother at the fragile age of sixteen. Determined to rise above life's challenges, she graduated from Troy University with a Bachelor of Science degree having studied Business and Psychology. Franchesca has modestly and successfully built her own financial literacy business, focusing on taxes, credit, training, and consulting. She also discerningly coaches other business owners on how to achieve the same success by prioritizing and creating the balance they desire between their personal and professional lives.

Franchesca is a certified tax professional (ASFP credentialed) and a board-certified Q1 Credit Consultant. She is a member of the Credit Consultants Association (CCA).

She is the principal of *Common Cents Solutions*. In this role, Franchesca manages a team of tax professionals, credit specialists, and business consultants, providing all aspects of financial literacy, including individual and business taxes, consumer and commercial credit, business operations, and management. She is highly customer-centric with superlative relationship building skills as evidenced by achievement in building six-figure annual sales and more than six hundred (600) new customer accounts in the past four (4) years, primarily through referrals. Her self-confidence, determination, dedication, organization, and motivation paired with tenacious sales and marketing skills have provided a solid foundation for new business and cultivating existing customer relationships.

A philanthropist at heart, her passion is what led to her long career and thriving business in empowering men and women alike, to regain financial stability and reclaim their independence. Driven still, after more than 20 years of working with consumer and financial services industries, she has committed to paper her debuting no-nonsense self-help book: *Making Common Cents of Credit*.

While Franchesca enjoys giving back to her community, conducting workshops, creating educational platforms, and speaking at various events, she relishes every moment she gets to share with family and friends. She currently resides in the city of natural beauty – Wetumpka, Alabama –with her husband and children.

BOOK MANTRA

I am an advocate for financial literacy and entrepreneurship. I also believe that anyone can achieve success and still have a happy balanced life. My mission is to embrace, empower, and elevate men and women to become financially independent and to overcome shame issues and other personal obstacles by leveraging their key resources. In my business, I help consumers, aspiring entrepreneurs, entrepreneurs, corporate professionals, and non-profits to realize their dreams. I am also a public speaker, author, philanthropist, mentor, and educator. I hope to be able to work with you to fill the financial literacy gap.

Links and Social Media Info

Website: www.franchesca.org
Instagram: instagram.com/makingcommoncents
Facebook: Facebook.com/FranchescaRoss-Jones
LinkedIn: Linkedin.com/in/FranchescaRoss
Twitter.com: Twitter.com/FranchescaRoss9

Equipped To Win

Sheraton Gatlin

"For God hath not given us the spirit of fear; but of power,
and of love, and of a sound mind."
- 2 Timothy 1:7 (King James Version)

"Not that I speak in respect of want: for I have learned,
in whatsoever state I am, therewith to be content."
- Philippians 4:11

Many situations tend to transpire in life, both good and bad and seem to occur when we least expect them. Human nature has become fearful, stressed, or caused to develop some disabilities such as anxiety or depression. How can we really prepare for these harsh moments? I do not think any country of the world was truly prepared for such a shift in relation to the COVID-19 pandemic. So many parts of our lives changed and will remain changed forever. Some of the individuals of the world were impacted directly while others were indirect. However, every one of us has been impacted in some way. This moment in our lives is truly an experience we won't forget.

The great news is that even in a pandemic, you can still claim *Victory* this season. What is even better is that you already have the necessary tools and resources to do it – to win! You are fully equipped to do exactly what God has positioned and purposed for you to do.

I wondered about the future, just like everyone else when the pandemic hit. How was this going to alter my life, corporate job, business, income, and my ability to continue being an active boss mom? I still had upcoming projects to finish. I had upcoming makeup appointments. I had planned events to attend. *How could this change all of that?* I questioned. I will never forget trying to beat the crowds to the grocery store in attempt to prevent going without. The initial change that impacted my life was when my corporate job made the decision for my department to begin working from home. This was quite a transition and only the beginning. The second change that impacted my life was when I had to discontinue my plans to travel to see my son for spring break, which I typically do every year. This was the first time I was not going to be able to spend spring break with him. Talk about heartbreaking, especially when you are already miles apart. Shortly thereafter, the pandemic impacted my personal business as an entrepreneur. The opportunities and jobs to do makeup became scarce. Events were now being prohibited, establishments closed, and social distancing enforced. I then began to ponder on "Where do I go from here?"

Regardless of what was going on around me, I still felt in my Spirit that God did not bring me this far to leave me. I had to take a moment to reflect, focus, and let God minister to me. I had to shift from negative thinking to positive thinking, which I also encourage you to do, Queen. The mind is a powerful thing, and if you do not grab hold of your thoughts to control them, they will control you. I began to reflect on my gifts and projects that I already completed, relationships that were already built, merchandise I had already invested in, and consideration for my sense of self. I began to look at the pandemic as the perfect opportunity for triumph.

I was blessed to still be working my job full-time. But, how would I supplement the lost income, pay bills, and finish my upcoming projects? I stopped looking at my losses and considered the gains. I had been presented with the opportunity to be a co-author in not only one, but two books, *Pray, Slay, and COLLECT* as well as *BOSS MOMS*. Not only was I fortunate enough to inspire, and make money at the same time, I was concerned about finishing my personal memoir with no additional income due to the reduced hours in business. The next thing I know, my company offered access to our 401K plans due to the pandemic, talk about divine timing. I was willing to take a short term risk for a lifetime of royalties. Needless to say, I was able to release my memoir, and pay up some bills. My credit score increased, and I have money in all my accounts. You can too, Sis! To put the icing on the cake, I was able to invest in my first product, lip balm for VoirBelle LLC. We have to remember that no matter what it looks like, there is a blessing in the storm. I am actually in a better position than I was prior to the pandemic. I truly believe I was positioned to *win*. And not only *win* in this season but forever. God wants us to win and live life abundantly, so don't let the enemy trick you into thinking anything different.

Although I transitioned to working from home, the blessing was not only that I still had a job, but I felt even more privileged with the ability to easier manage my day for work, home, and business life. I could now truly set a positive tone to start my day and maintain it throughout. I began to start each day with a sermon. Taking the time to not only be fed by the Word of God, but fall into worship and thank God for what He has done. I began to write positive affirmations and manifestations daily with the encouragement to do so from a friend. If for any reason I fail to write them, I speak them to be sure they go out into the atmosphere. I practice prioritizing my day so I ensure I work on my dreams and remain productive. To ensure my dreams come true, I continue working towards them every day, even during such a time as this. I focus more on my sense of self, peace, and doing those things that make me happy. And now that I have been able to travel and get my son, working from home has afforded me a greater opportunity to spend more time with him this summer.

This is the perfect time for you to understand your purpose, walk in your purpose, and do what God has called you to do. Consider this downtime as the best time to work on being the divine you, so you can come out of this pandemic on top. That may be by investing in a business or simply investing in you. It may be by being a better mom, sister, grandmother, auntie, or friend. But, whatever it is, do it while you have plenty of time. You may want to learn something new or sharpen a skill set. What better time than now? Why are you delaying being a better queen?

While asking God to order your steps, I encourage you to plan your week and then your days to maximize it. Find a method that works for you. This may be by writing your to-do list down, using a calendar, setting alarms, jotting down reminders on a white board, texting yourself, or even using a third-party app to help you keep a checklist. I can only tell you from experience that all of these methods have assisted me in managing my day and checking off my goals. I suggest utilizing this time to cultivate methods on how to be better personally whether that be spiritually, mentally, emotionally, physically, or all. I suggest educating yourself more in relation to your business or craft as this can also aid in your being one step closer to your dreams. If you keep God first, exercise the gifts you possess, and believe, faith will take you a long way. I encourage you to continue to increase your knowledge, prioritize tasks, practice time management, and speak into the atmosphere, calling those things that are not, as if they were already. Be not fearful, but instead be ye ready. Know that you have everything you need, Queen, to *win* in this season.

About the Author:

Sheraton Gatlin is a published international celebrity makeup artist enhancing the beauty within people all around the world. She is a #1 International Best-Selling Author/3x Best Selling author who has achieved numerous accomplishments inside and outside of the beauty industry. You can also catch her in the latest series on iTunes as an actress in "Thick Skin".

Sheraton Gatlin

www.voirbelle.com

VoirBelle LLC.

IG: @voirbelle

FB: VoirBelle by Sheraton

404-333-1529

P.R.E.S.S. to Win

Eboni Montsho

"I sought the Lord, and He heard me,
and delivered me from all my fears."
Psalm 34:4 KJV

So shall my word be that goeth forth out of my mouth: it shall not return unto
me void, but it shall accomplish that which I please, and it shall prosper in the
thing whereto I sent it.
Isaiah 55:11 KJV

When you hear the word PRESS, what comes to mind? If you are like me, an image of someone pushing down on a hard surface is what you see. You may think of grapes being "pressed" during the winemaking process or if you are a millennial, you think about pressed in the sense of "I'm pressed," which means I am mad or bothered. If you have teens or millennials around you and they tell you, "You are pressing me or I'm pressed," you have gotten on their last nerve.

Moving forward, when you hear the word PRESS, I want you to still associate the definition and image of applying pressure because you are mad, bothered or agitated by something or someone. However, I want the "way" you PRESS to look and feel different.

You may have endured several struggles, fought battles, and persevered through numerous days of what seemed to be an endless flow of tears and pain. Some days, you find yourself crying out, "God, when will it be my turn? When will I be able to wake up without a feeling of emptiness, fear, sadness, grief, shame, or guilt?" In fact, you are saying to yourself, "I am ready to feel happy, satisfied, fulfilled, and content."

My sister, my brother, I hear you. God hears you. It is no accident or coincidence you are reading this book. It is your time to win! It is time to PRESS differently. Let's take a look at a 5-step PRESS process to use during the difficult moments of life that will shift your mental state:

P – Posture
During the crisis moments of life, what is your posture?
The way you handle adversity is key in your growth journey. Let me give you a small secret right now, adversity will always be a part of your life. Get used to it. The types of challenges you face may change, but you will always have a challenge to face. However, while you are going through adversity, what is your posture? Picture this, the game is being played, and you have been on the bench the whole season. Some of your teammates have fouled out, a fight even broke out and a team member was kicked out the game, the star player has missed several important shots, and even one of the starting line-up players who has your same position was injured last game, so they are out for the rest of the season, still the coach has not put you in

the game. Things are happening around you and to you, both good and bad, but you are still sitting on the bench of life. God has not moved you. In moments like this, what does your posture look like?

Posture is defined as a way of dealing with or considering something, an approach or attitude. When you have a purposeful posture, i.e., attitude, it requires intentionality, focus and commitment. What are your goals for the next six months? What are you passionate about? Take a moment and create a visual image that represents the posture it will take to accomplish your six-month goal plan.

Every time you feel yourself about to have a pity party, look at the posture picture you drew. Every time you are ready to throw in the towel, look at the posture picture. The Bible records in Luke, chapter 8, a woman who lived twelve long years of her life with an issue of blood that was incurable by local physicians. She changed her posture, pressed her way to Jesus, and was made whole. Her posture was filled with determination, courage, and obedience.

R - Response
During the crisis moments of life, what is your response?
I was in abusive relationships one after another for over twelve years. I did drugs, drank alcohol, and self-destructed great paying jobs. I struggled with insecurities, anger, and unforgiveness. In the past, I would curse, speak to others with an abundant amount of sarcasm, I gave up easily, procrastinated, and even refused to go where I knew God was sending me. Now, I understand why Jonah had a hard time going to Nineveh (Jonah 1). Can you relate? The way you respond to adversity will either allow you to be free or continue to keep you in bondage. Respond in love and continue to trust in God. He will heal you, restore you, and make you whole. Life is a battle, and we are soldiers.

Every morning I want you to get up and suit up for battle. Most often than not, you are fighting yourself. Remain focused on the journey. This battle is not your first victory. Think about how you overcame the last one. The more you focus on positivity you will feel comfortable with taking on challenges that may have previously been outside of your comfort zone. On this winning journey, along the path I like to call *the road-less-traveled*, you will discover your authentic self. You will be a game changer!

E – Encouragement

During the crisis moments of life, who encourages you?

One of my mentees called me about a week or so ago and said to me, "Coach, you pour out so much to us, and you are always feeding our spirits. Who encourages you?" I had to really stop and think about this question before answering. In that moment, I was reminded how critical and necessary, encouragement is in my faith walk. The Bible tells us in, 1 Thessalonians 5:11, to encourage one another and build one another up. As human beings, it is important to hear "you got this," "keep pushing," "I see you boo," "you killing it," "you are goal smashing," or similar phrases because they will keep you motivated to finish strong.

S – Seek

During the crisis moments of life, who/what do you seek?

At one point in my life, I sought vices to ease the pain. If you want your pain to truly stop and come to an end, you must seek God. Psalms 34:4 (NRSV) says, *"I sought the Lord, and he answered me, and delivered me from all my fears."* Seek Him because He can give you something that you cannot give yourself. He can give you love, peace, joy, and happiness. Seek Him while He can yet be found.

S – SPEAK

During the crisis moments of life, what do you speak to yourself?
It is your words that provide a bold confirmation of your innermost thoughts. You learn what you think of yourself and others through your choice of words. When you continue to repeat the same words and thoughts, they become truth. Not only in your mind, but in the minds of others as well. Henry Ford once said, "Whether you think you can, or you think you can't—you're right."

Do you currently use words such as *can't, never,* or *won't,* always? If you do, please remove them from your vocabulary. These words strip you of your ability to manifest the life that you want to live. The next time you find yourself about to speak negatively about yourself, I want you to answer these 3 questions:

- Why am I thinking this way?
- How will this line of thinking help me move forward?
- What statements of healing can I speak instead?

Psalmist would say, *"Let the words of my mouth, and the meditation of my heart, be acceptable in thy sight, O LORD, my strength, and my redeemer"* (Psalms 19:14 KJV).

You have the power to speak to your own mountain and tell it to be removed. Mark 11:23 validates that the mountain will move if you *do not doubt in your heart* but believe that it will come to pass. One amazingly effective tool you can use to create statements of healing, are affirmations. Affirmations are positive statements that can help to challenge and overcome self-sabotaging and negative thoughts. When repeated often, the words begin to infiltrate your thoughts which ultimately would change your behavior. *"So shall my word be that goes out from my mouth; it shall not return to me empty, but it shall accomplish that which I purpose, and shall succeed in the thing for which I sent it" (Isaiah 55:11 ESV).*

Here are a few statements of hope and healing you can speak when negative thoughts and feelings begin to consume you:

- I will live a life of abundance and financial overflow.
- Everyone connected to me shall have what is decreed.
- My heart and mind are at peace, and unity follows me.
- I am strengthened by God's power and full of His love.
- I have everything I need inside of me to WIN.
- I am perfect just as I am.
- All things are working together for my good.

Identify one place you are feeling hopeless, helpless, or defeated, and in need of God's help. Find a scripture and repeat it every day or repeat one of the affirmations listed above.

Your faith will begin to grow, and transformation will happen. Behold, Jesus has given you authority to tread on serpents and scorpions, and over all the power of the enemy and nothing shall hurt you! Win! Woman, win! Go forth and P.R.E.S.S., until you are made whole.

About the Author:
Eboni Montsho is committed to guiding others to overcome their past, discover their purpose, and unleash their personal power. She provides ready-to-use principles that result in your divorcing your excuses, eliminating mental roadblocks, and creating a unique action plan designed for goal-smashing success.

Eboni Montsho, a native of Chicago, Illinois, is an empowerment speaker, accountability coach, author, and purpose pusher. She has been featured in *Rolling Out Magazine* and seen on CBS, NBC, and FOX, to name a few. Eboni brings more than fifteen years of human resources and leadership experience to every engagement, having worked in corporate, nonprofit, government, and faith-based environments. She uses her master's degrees in Human Resources Management and Business Administration to coach, counsel, and guide her clients to discover personal accountability.

WEBSITE:
www.ebonimontsho.com
SOCIAL MEDIA HANDLES:
FB - Eboni Montsho Ignites
IG - EboniMontshoIgnites

My L.I.F.E (Living in Faith Everyday)

Vanessa L. Foulks

"I shall not die, but live, and declare the works of the LORD."
Psalm 118:17 (KJV)

When you have a higher purpose on this earth, you cannot just die. God has saved my life over and over again. Like when I was sixteen years old on a basketball court and witnessed a guy being shot in the head. Then, the shooter turned the gun to my head, and the gun jammed. Or when I was deployed to Iraq and my vehicle did not roll over the improvised explosive device, but the truck that followed my truck rolled over the explosive and all the passengers died. Or when I wanted to take my own life because the pressure of being raped by my supervisor weighed heavily on me, but my three-year-old son called, and I lowered my handgun from my mouth. No matter what has happened in my life, God has saved me over and over again. Sometimes, it may take you looking back over your life to realize that those times that seemed the worst, had God always ready for you. My strong, positive will to live and overcome sustains and sees me through, only by the grace of God.

Matthew 22:14 (KJV): "For many are called, but few are chosen."

I grew up in the church, but my relationship and dependency on God did not develop until I became an adult. I have always been told that God would use me to heal other's hurt, but I did not understand what that entailed. I have learned throughout my life that people who are healers have endured certain situations of heartbreak, illness, abuse, poverty, and/or depression, which can only be helped by a person that would not only understand but would speak healing over their person. I am the called, the few and chosen for such a time as this. With the world in an uproar over illness, racism, oppression, and poverty, God is calling all healers to their position. As a child and a teenager, I never took the prophecy given to me so often, seriously. I did not know what it meant, to be honest. Yes, I believed in God and yes, I saw miracles happen in church. I saw the people that would pray so hard they would disregard things happening around them, and I knew I did not want that to be me. Due to the long hours that these *healing sessions* would take, the church was quickly becoming not for me: "When I am grown, I'm not going to church, and I'm not going to make my children go." It felt like more of a punishment than a privilege to go to church. Maybe it was that I was living off my mother's relationship with God. Maybe it was that I could not *enjoy my life* because I was always in church. Or maybe it was all the rules developed by humans that had nothing to do with the Word of God that made me feel the church was not for me. God never changes his mind about you, though. Listen, I have run from God and the things that I know I should be doing, but was always led right back to the path.

The military was the most challenging season of my life. Dealing with racism, sexism, rape, and financial struggles, all the while raising two sons by myself, should have taken my mind or my life. Even to this day, as I recall different portions of that time, I cannot do anything but accept the calling of God in my life. Why me Lord, why do I need to go through this pain? Hopefully, as you continue to read, you will find tools to benefit you in accepting your purpose and call for your life: if not you, then who?

2 Timothy 2:3-4 (NKJV): You, therefore, must endure hardship as a good soldier of Jesus Christ. No one engaged in warfare entangles himself with the affairs of this life, that he may please him who enlisted him as a soldier.

Do you know that you are a soldier? Whether you serve for positive or negative outcomes, you still war for a specific mission, and that makes you a soldier. While in the military, I learned that I am accountable for the gear that is assigned to me. Whether that be my weapon, my uniform, my duties, or my conduct, I am held accountable for it all. I am thankful for all lessons learned in the Military, because I use these lessons as my accountability tool for my life today. Every tear shed and every pain felt was a part of my arsenal of tools to not only survive in life, but to thrive in it. The tools that have helped me to make it in life are gratitude, reconciliation, alignment, commitment, and endurance (G.R.A.C.E).

2 Corinthians 12:9 (KJV): My grace is sufficient for thee: for my strength is made perfect in weakness.

day I would go through my G.R.A.C.E period. This period was a tangible action that allowed me to get out of my bouts of depression and anxiety. It took my mind off the everyday thoughts of hating my life the way it was and focusing on healing. The healing of current and past traumas is what set me free. In times of weakness, grace made me strong.

Intentional gratitude can be written or unwritten. Twice a day, every morning and every night, I write a list of everything that I am grateful for, no matter how small. *I am so grateful for my eyes to see, my ears to hear, my blood and bones, hands, and feet.* Showing gratitude changes your thought process from lack to gain. It reminds you of all the goodness that you have in life and minimizes the thoughts of need. There were times when I could not think of anything to write because the bills were due, and there was no money anywhere in sight. I opened my journal and read out loud my list from days, before repeating them over and over again. In minutes I would feel a sense of relief and peace come over me like everything was already worked out.

Reconcile with your past. This can be done by reflecting on the mistakes in your past and forgive yourself. Forgive yourself from the disappointment from your parents, the heartbreaks from lost loves, and from all the things you have regretted doing in your lifetime. My reconciliation came when I had to forgive myself for how I raised my sons. I have two sons that I feel I did everything I could to raise them right. I was a single mom. I couldn't afford football games and senior trips, so my sons didn't go to many events while in school. The guilt of not being able to give them all the things children should experience has sat with me for years. I felt ashamed they didn't have the average life as their friends. One day, while writing in my journal, I received a text from my son, thanking me for being the best mom I could be and showing him love every day of his life. Sometimes, the best we have is just enough for what's needed, forgive yourself.

Alignment, according to Webster's dictionary, means an arrangement in a straight line, or correct or appropriate relative positions. It's time that I aligned myself. I knew that God would meet me where I was if I did the right thing. I created a budget so that I could see where my money was going to avoid getting into positions I could not resolve. I got into a route of discipline in my eating and exercising; getting up for early meditation and prayer and most of all, aligning my thoughts. The battle was in my mind. I knew I could be and do better than where I was, but my thoughts kept me captive.

Commitment and endurance go together. Once you take the steps to be grateful for what you have, forgive yourself for the past and commit to being the best version of yourself, then you will be able to endure through whatever comes your way. Please understand that these acts of grace were not the cure-all to my problems. I still have problems; however, I can quickly resolve or devise a plan to function amid them.

In the Yoruban tradition of Ifa/Orisha, the concept of good character is Iwa-Pele (e-wah-peh-Leh), this is what people in this religion strive for every day. Good character shows that what you believe is something higher than yourself that will allow you to deal with the issues of life. It is being the best person you can be to yourself, others, nature, and the earth. In keeping with the theme of this book and the reason for it, I believe that no matter what comes your way, you can win. Your trauma was not for you, but for those that come after you, those that follow you. Imagine the things you are going through now, and then imagine a woman that meets you on the other side of your trial, and how you can draw a map for her to win. So, get your journal and write the vision and make it plain, so that others can hear your story of gratitude, reconciliation, alignment, commitment, and endurance.

About the Author:

Vanessa L Foulks is CEO of Healthy Foulks, a multi-faceted company promoting a healthy mental, spiritual, financial, and physical life. She is a decorated United States Army veteran that proudly served for fourteen years as a Senior Non-Commissioned Officer until separating in 2014. She has a bachelor's degree in Healthcare Administration, a master's degree in Christian Ministry, and is currently pursuing a Doctor of Strategic Leadership with concentration in Healthcare Leadership. She is a speaker and advocate of suicide prevention and sexual abuse prevention. She believes that by telling her own story of wrestling with suicide and overcoming sexual abuse, she can help someone to heal, and have a healthy mental, spiritual, and emotional life. Vanessa is married to the Rev. Brian Foulks and together they have a blended family with five children.

Other work: Unleashing the Roar: I am My Sister's Keeper
www.unleashingtheroar.com/vanessa-singleton

OVERCOME YOUR FEARS

Miesha Henderson

"And the LORD, he it is that doth go before thee; he will be with thee, he will not fail thee, neither forsake thee: fear not, neither be dismayed."
Deuteronomy 31:8 KJV

"Be careful for nothing; but in every thing by prayer and supplication with thanksgiving let your requests be made known unto God. And the peace of God, which passeth all understanding, shall keep your hearts and minds through Christ Jesus."
Philippians 4:6-7 KJV

Fear Gets You Nowhere

Have you ever sat down and thought about an idea and said, "Yasssss! That's the million-dollar idea right there. This idea will make millions." But then, you don't do anything about it because you are focused on thoughts like, what if others do not like my idea? What if I don't make money? Will I receive support from my peers?

Where do I start? I am scared to start because I might fail. If you have, then know you are not alone. That was exactly how I felt.

Starting Sisters Empowerment Movement was the scariest decision I have ever made. Besides, who was I to try to empower women knowing that I needed empowering myself. See, I suffer from depression and often times, I've felt so low I could barely get out of bed in the morning, let alone trying to encourage someone else. In addition, I had a problem with my own self confidence. I thought I wasn't good enough or worthy enough to become a motivational speaker. In my head, a motivational speaker was someone that spoke properly, had a huge following, and was an influencer.

I had a dream that I would be talking to the majority, even though I don't speak properly, have no huge fan base, and wasn't an influencer. I do, however, influence the people around me, and that was it. I influence the people in my circle, my family and friends. My first event brought over seventy people and became a huge success. If I would have let fear get in the way, I would have never started. See, what God has for you is for you and no one else. You can be in a field that's oversaturated, but if God led you to it, then He will make room for you.

No need to be afraid of something that is your God-given purpose. All I ask is that you give whatever you do one hundred percent. You can't sit and ask God for a miracle or favor when you haven't put in any work. Saint Augustine says, "Pray as though everything depended on God. Work as though everything depended on you." Put yourself in the position to win. James 2:26 (KJV) says, *"For as the body without the spirit is dead, so faith without works is dead also."*
Don't let fear get in the way of your dreams, goals, or success. Do the work and everything else will fall into place.

You can still have a Full-time job

While starting this organization, I still worked a full time job and often thought it's just meant for me to work that job and take care of my family, and that's it. I wasn't satisfied with that outcome, so I started working on my business after work. I made the time. I knew that in order to start Sisters Empowerment Movement, I had to speak with other women who were in the same field and had knowledge of how to host events. I faced a lot of obstacles, including questioning whether I would be able to find an affordable location for the event. How would I market? Was anyone going to come to the event? How much was this event going to cost?

I had to do some research, which I realized was not going to happen overnight. I had to have patience and know that with God I can do all things. I realized what set me apart from the rest as well as what set Sisters Empowerment Movement apart from others, was what we offered our community. My events are designed to empower women with self-love and self-care, to embrace who they are and to receive health awareness, fitness goals, inspirational advice, and more. You'll definitely experience an exceptional, empowering, intrinsic discovery of yourself and the beauty within. No matter who you are, you are to be celebrated and loved.

Even though you have a full time job, you can still find time to work at your business. I always say, if it's important to you, you will find a way. If it's not important to you, you will find an excuse.

Winning this Season

I wanted to take my vision a step further. This year, I decided to get my life coach certification because not only did I want to call myself a motivational speaker or the founder of Sisters Empowerment Movement, I also wanted to make sure I had the credentials behind it. I suffer from the imposter syndrome. An imposter syndrome is the persistent inability to believe that one's success is deserved or has been legitimately achieved as a result of one's own efforts or skills. Even though I have coached many women and all of my friends call me a life coach, I wasn't comfortable with stating that to others, because remember, I am the same person that has an issue with self-confidence. I wanted to get this certification for myself in order to be comfortable with telling others, I am a life coach. This was a part of God's plan. But I had to put in the work, go to class and invest in my future. Paying the money for this certification was an investment. Before this, I was in my head, often talking myself out of a lot of things because of fear that maybe, I would not be a good life coach. Maybe I would not get any clients after I've received my certification. Fear of where do I go from here. Fear of what is my niche. But I've had my niche all along. I am a confidence-coach.

Since I have dealt with this personally, and I have the platform ready, this is what I do. I help women discover their confidence by empowering them to embrace their individuality and accept their true selves. I help women achieve their goals. No goal is too big or too small. I give women the resources they need to continue to succeed in life, all the while doing this respectfully and with integrity.

I wanted to come out of COVID-19 having learned new things and not being the same as I was before the pandemic. I had to keep evolving. I still wanted to connect with my peers and offer some encouragement and help during this trying time. I started having *Zoom* sessions to deal with the anxiety during this time. I have hosted zoom sessions about financial literacy and becoming debt-free. At this point, I still had fear, but then I changed my outlook as if I was giving a service and sharing valuable information. If it was meant for the person to be on the conference call, then they would be on the call. Even if it was only one person who joined, that one person will learn something from it.

I started receiving thanks for having these meetings. People were expressing the meetings were informative and were asking when the next meetings would occur. After that confirmation, I knew I had to keep going. I also started selling Sisters Empowerment Movement face mask and t-shirts with different slogans. I started sending cash apps to essential workers who were following me on social media.

Overcoming Fear

Fear gets you nowhere. Fear had stopped me from doing so many things I could have done earlier. I had to stop and ask myself, "What is the fear? What is holding you back?" I had to resist the urge to quit because, even though things do get hard, one has to keep going. The main conqueror of my fear was Deuteronomy 31:8 (KJV) which says, *"And the Lord, he it is that doth go before thee: he will be with thee, he will not fail thee, neither forsake thee: fear not, neither be dismayed."*

Once I came to the Lord with my problems and fear, He showed me He would be with me and not fail me. So, there is no need to fear. The Lord is with you. When you go to the Lord, all things will work out in His will. For Philippians 4:6-7 (KJV) says, *"Be careful for nothing; but in everything by prayer and supplication with thanksgiving let your request be made known unto God. And the peace of God, which passeth all understanding, shall keep your hearts and minds through Christ Jesus."*

My Tips for winning
- The first thing you need to know is that you determine your own destiny.
- Believe in yourself.
- Pray for your purpose.
- Philippians 4:6-7 (KJV): *"Be careful for nothing; but in everything by prayer and supplication with thanksgiving let your request be made*

44

known unto God. And the peace of God, which passeth all understanding, shall keep your hearts and minds through Christ Jesus."

- Speak your dreams into existence.
- Don't ever give up. Believe me, I know it's hard especially when things may not go as fast as you would like, but you have to keep going.
- If someone says No, be curious to find out the reason for their No.
- Invest in yourself.
- Have faith.
- Get out of your comfort zone.
- Fear gets you nowhere; have no fear.
- Deuteronomy 31:8 (KJV) says *"And the Lord, he it is that doth go before thee: he will be with thee, he will not fail thee, neither forsake thee: fear not, neither be dismayed."*
- Write it down and make it plain.
- Make a plan and stick to it.
- Think about why you've started.
- Be consistent.
- Starve your Distractions.
- Resist the urge to quit.
- Know that all things are possible with Christ.

Long story short, you must overcome fear and know that you can do whatever it is you put your mind to, as long as you have Christ by your side.

About Sisters Empowerment Movement:

Sisters Empowerment Movement is an organization dedicated to providing encouragement and motivation to women. We specialize in empowering, encouraging, motivating, building confidence, promoting self-love, self-care, and networking. We are known for bringing awareness to mental health and uplifting one another.

Sisters Empowerment Movement can be reached at:
Instagram: www.instagram.com/sistersempowermentmovement
Facebook:
https://www.facebook.com/groups/sistersempowermentmovement

WHEN PRINCE CHARMING LEFT

Godella Petty

"Fear not; for thou shalt not be ashamed: neither be thou confounded; for thou shalt not be put to shame: for thou shalt forget that shame of thy youth, and shalt not remember the reproach of thy widowhood any more. For they Maker is thine husband; the LORD of host is his name; and thy Redeemer the Holy One of Israel; The God of the whole earth shall he be called."
Isaiah 54:4-5

"And be not conformed of this world but be ye transformed by the renewing of your mind, that ye may prove what is that good, and acceptable, and perfect, will of God."
Romans 12:2

In the beginning, you thought that love would come and grab you by the heart and pull you to run with it. Being out there looking for love in all the places you thought was right, could leave you in a situation of total chaos, and you keep on running. You must be so incredibly careful of the enemy's traps when you are looking for your Prince Charming. That one person you think is designed for you could be the person that was sent to throw you off the course of your destiny.

The Bible says in Romans 12:2 (KJV): *"And be not conformed of this world but be ye transformed by the renewing of your mind, that ye may prove what is that good, and acceptable, and perfect, will of God."* So many times we are so going hot about love, Mr. Wonderful or Prince Charming, that we end up leaning on our own understanding and not consulting God to lead us. We must strive for the perfect will of God even in our love life. Some men can make you believe that you have this great romantic relationship, and you will fall for it, almost all the time.

There is nothing wrong with giving someone a chance to prove their love. When many fall into trap is when they go against what is good and acceptable. It is never acceptable to go against the will of God. Being a believer, there are commandments that we must adhere to. And when we fall short there are some consequences that we may have to go through. Yes, we serve an amazingly forgiving God, but we also know that we have consequences when it comes to not allowing God's will to be done. This applies to all areas of life.

When Prince Charming left, it was a great fall, so you may think. But you have to know that all a person put you through could be a sign that he is not the one for you. Any one that will have you compromise your walk with Christ is one that you need to stay away from. *"For God so loved the world, that He gave His only begotten Son, that whoever believes in Him should not perish but have everlasting life"* (John 3:16 NKJV). No one is worth that and no one can give you that. Be mindful like the Word say and lean not on your own understanding of your life.

As we go through life, we have to know that we have purpose. However, we have to be wary of the enemy who comes to steal, kill and destroy (John 10:10). So many times we get wrapped up in the ways of the world that we miss the mark of looking out for our souls. Being in what we think is love will cause great pain, if we are not careful to observe and evade the tactics the enemy throws constantly at us. We have to get and stay armored up, covering our self, and not just the head or the feet but our whole self. Do you know that the enemy can take that same love that we crave so much for and fashion something so tragic?

Listen, being a woman that gives her all to a man that only kept on demanding and taking is an extremely tiring task. It is so ugly, as one may not know one could have more or even deserve more. God is so faithful and will bring you to your senses, if you allow Him. Believing that giving up a child is the best because Prince Charming said he didn't want any more children is not of God. Simply thinking about all these signs should bring you into a place of worship, into closeness to your God. Why? This is because it is God's pull on you to Himself, moreover, you are yet to tell your story to others that may be going down the same road, which is a blessing in itself. For we are blessed to be a blessing:

> *Fear not; for thou shalt not be ashamed: neither be thou confounded; for thou shalt not be put to shame: for thou shalt forget that shame of thy youth, and shalt not remember the reproach of thy widowhood any more. For they Maker is thine husband; the LORD of host is his name; and thy Redeemer the Holy One of Israel; The God of the whole earth shall he be called.* (Isaiah 54:4-5)

We must know that even though, the enemy comes and pushes us into areas of ungodly thoughts and deeds, we don't have to be ashamed because God said He would forgive the shame of our youth. Your youth could be when you were four, fifteen, or twenty-three years old and yes, even your yesterday could be your *youth*. Trust God. Give Him your old being and watch how He will make you anew. See the leaving of Prince Charming as the opened door to new things. It opened door to a new way of thinking, a new way of living, and a new way of receiving and giving love. You will win if you only believe and strive hard for a new life with God.

Do you know there is nothing you have done or can do that could separate you from the love of Christ? You don't have to reminisce on how awful things were in your life. The Bible says in Philippians 4:8:

> Finally, brethren whatsoever things are true, whatsoever things are honest, whatsoever things are just, whatsoever things are pure, whatsoever things are lovely, whatsoever things are of good report; if there be any virtue, and if there be any praise, think on these things.

Isn't that great? Do not let the ways of this world have you thinking you are not worthy or just messed up so much that nothing will get better. Of course, things can get better, and yes, they will.

Maybe when Prince Charming Left, he took everything; he cleaned out the bank account and took all the possessions. Maybe not only that, but that he had continued his relationship with the women he was cheating with during the marriage. See, Prince Charming could be dating the neighbor as well as his friend's daughter who call him uncle. This is because the enemy will twist the minds of anyone that allow him to, just like that of Prince Charming. Prince Charming doesn't care that you are in a wheel chair with a broken ankle and not able to fend for yourself or your children. He just walked away with everything, not giving a second thought to all effort you may have put into making the house a home for both of you, or what you and your children would eat as he knows you have no money or food.

I tell you, God is so wonderful that in the process of restoration he will give you all that you need. He will give you the ability to gather resources to take care of you and your children. He will allow supernatural healing not only in your mind and body but in your soul as well. Being delivered of the demonic soul-ties of Prince Charming will give you a profound new way of thinking and living. There is no greater power than allowing the Holy Spirit to take over and have His way in your life. When the enemy comes in like a flood, the Spirit of the Lord will lift up a standard against him.

It's easy for a person to think on the ugly things of life such as this and be down and out. It is easier, but you must remember, to take those tragic mishaps and begin to ask God: "How is this going to be for my good? What do you have me do with all this that I have gone through? You said in your word that I am more than a conquer?" At this stage, you have to tell God His word. The Bible says that His word cannot come back to Him void (Isaiah 55:11). As you talk to Him, let Him know you may be having a difficult time redirecting the hurtful thoughts of your past. He will listen, and He most surely will answer. Just believe and pray. Both go together.

Do not believe that all is lost because you have been ransomed to win. You are a winner. It is so pleasing to welcome the leaving of devilish Prince Charming and be free. Some goodbyes will have you in tears but for a moment. Remember, joy comes in the morning. And it surely was morning, when Prince Charming Left.

About the Author:

Godelly Petty is a mother, an author, evangelist, advocate, and a motivational speaker. She is the founder of two wonderful organizations located in Milwaukee, Wisconsin: *The Professional Advocacy LLC* offers supervised visitation to parent with children that have been placed in out-of-home care. We also help with advocating for veterans, foster children, and families that need assistance.

The second is the *Sons and Daughters of Virtue Outreach Ministry*, a nonprofit organization that helps with food, housing, and other resources to better the lives of our clients. We offer credit repair and business opportunities to those that want to secure entrepreneurship.

You can connect with Petty on:

Facebook: Mary Angel
Instagram: MaryAngel1019
Website: www.themaryangel.weebly.com

Road Closed, Detour Ahead

Yoeshikoe Creer

"And not only this, but we also exult in our tribulations, knowing that tribulation brings about perseverance; and perseverance, proven character; and proven character, hope; and hope does not disappoint, because the love of God has been poured out within our hearts through the Holy Spirit who was given to us."
Romans 5:3-5 NASB

"And we know that God causes all things to work together for good to those who love God, to those who are called according to His *purpose. "*
Romans 8:28 NASB

We, at times, can be very impatient. We want our lives and plans to be so uninterrupted that whenever we come to a detour in our travels, we rarely take the time to consider whether the detour has a purpose. Most times, detours are annoying and impact our emotions heavily, even if momentarily. I admit detours can be frustrating, but if we follow them with patience they will bring us to our appointed time that will satisfy rather than disappoint us.

I recall a time I was driving through a country road, taking a route that I was familiar with, only to face a huge sign saying, "Road Closed, Detour Ahead." A road that I was pretty savvy driving on was now closed for repairs. I had hit a detour in my travel. Although I was not in a hurry, I still found myself not happy about taking an alternate route. Even though, I had lived in the area for a few years, I had never been forced to take a different road, except that particular day that detour was in effect. After all, detours do exist if there is construction taking place in order to fix or improve a road. So, as I took the right turn following the arrows, I began driving on newfound curvy road, the picturesque scene of which welcomed me just kilometers ahead. It was the most beautiful and striking group of homes and landscaping to live for. The trees and the greenery took my breath away. I had witnessed beautiful homes before, but nothing as powerful as that. It left me in awe.

Suddenly, it came to my mind that God had purposely sent me on this journey to bless me. His desire was to show me something different, and my spirit was so encouraged that day. It is amazing how a small inconvenience from God serves a true purpose of newness, peace and tranquility.

Similarly, God will take our personal lives on a detour, because He is constructing something in us. Of course, detours can be anything but convenient because they take us out of our way, and they, at times, make our destination a bit longer to reach, however, they are necessary.

Seemingly, I thought I had my year all planned out, but as I started on the familiar road in my life, I came to another single sign ahead, reading, "Road Closed, Detour Ahead." But, this time it was on a spiritual level. Although, 2020 has been a year full of detours after detours and after detours, it has still managed to usher in bountiful blessings in my life in which it has also added a great spiritual cleansing. Unexpected gifts from God continue to flow through my fingertips as I follow the arrows directing me when and where to turn. When God has a special place for us to be, He will add some alterations, twists, and turns in our lives. Just know that when God is leading us, we probably will not get there by going in a straight and narrow line.

We should immediately begin to humble ourselves and pray as we experience the detours in our lives. It is imperative to ask God for his guidance. We must be mentally, spiritually and emotionally available to the Lord's unexpected ways for our lives. Trust me, if you do, you will be in store for some blessings that you may have never expected nor anticipated. Romans 5:3-5 (NASB) says:

> *And not only this, but we also exult in our tribulations, knowing that tribulation brings about perseverance; and perseverance, proven character; and proven character, hope; and hope does not disappoint, because the love of God has been poured out within our hearts through the Holy Spirit who was given to us.*

"And we know that God causes all things to work together for good to those who love God, to those who are called according to His purpose" Romans 8:28 NASB.

About the Author:

Yoeshikoe Creer is a multi-published author, Ted X Marietta Square Speaker, mindfulness coach, and serial entrepreneur who enjoys spending quality time with her family in aquatic settings with tranquil views. Whether it be on boat or land, Yoeshikoe finds pleasure in natural scenery. Yoeshikoe thrives to inspire others to live good while living in their God-given purpose.

You can connect with Yoshi on:
IG: @Yoshicreerthewriter
Twitter: Yoshi Creer
FB: Yoeshikoe Nicole Creer

The Healing of Affliction

Dr. LaShonda M. Jackosn

"And he said unto her, Daughter,
thy faith hath made thee whole; go in peace, and be whole of thy plague."
Mark 5:34, KJV

What is success? It depends on who is answering the question because success can mean different things to different people as well as, different types of people. One agreeable definition of the term should be deciding on a goal, working towards it and actually achieving what you were working for, despite the odds. Success is measurable but the metrics are subjective and not determined by observers. There is always a story that precedes the win. Welcome to my story.

The image seen as Dr. LaShonda M. Jackson-Dean is one to be very proud of, but what about the time in life when the reflection was unbearable? It was year 1995 and the topic of discussion was how an individual found her selves in her current position? Dr. Jackson-Dean was a new Airman in the United States Airforce, still in the mist of getting to know who she was as a military person, as well as,

admitting what happened. She kept her house dark. She did not socialize beyond the necessary, slowly dying inside. This continued for years. She did everything she could to break out of that funk, but it had a death grip on her life.

Her breakthrough did not come, until she began to accept the things that she could not change. The main thing that she could not change was the thing that was holding her hostage, she was a rape victim. She finally said it. Her heart dropped. She felt herself sink to the floor. She laid there and cried. She cried until she could not cry any more, then she heard her own thoughts ask, "Now what?" She got off the floor, got on her knees and prayed. Every day, she would get on her knees and pray for healing, then she prayed for wisdom, and then for understanding. The last thing she prayed for was recovery. Good thing, she received all of what she asked for and in that order.

Fast forward to obtaining a few degrees, several certifications, accolades, successful businesses, marriage and children, she had made it through. She made it through with prayer and she finally remembered who she was. Would she have been the person she is today had she not had this traumatic experience? This can neither be confirmed nor denied, but the experience was definitely an awakening of her spirit. Before the incident, her observation was situation based. The incident that happened that night changed that in her. As horrid as it was, it caused her to become more aware of her surroundings and the participants of her environment. The new awareness retrained her focus which improved her interaction in future business deals. She persevered to earn her MBA, her Doctorate degree and several high-level certifications. Through it all, her path continued to lead towards servicing and assisting others. Whether it was through mentorship, coaching, or simply supporting, she was committed to helping others become more successful.

Dr. LaShonda Jackson-Dean is the CEO of Jackson-Dean Investments, the parent company for several other businesses including Jackson-Dean Professional Solutions; a life coaching practice for professional women. She also provides coaching services through her non-profit organization, Greatness Pursued, to women having difficulty in their transition from military to civilian life. The majority of these women also suffer from Military Sexual Trauma (MST). Under her leadership, Greatness Pursued has provided a safe place for the coaching of hundreds of women and basic living necessities for over three hundred other veterans.

Dr. Jackson-Dean is the author of five published books: A Phenomenological Study of the Underrepresentation of Senior Level African American Women in Corporations, Seed to Seeds Systemic Oppression and PTSD, Level Up! Through Mindfulness, Level Up! Through Mindfulness Life-Book Part II, and A Tea Party and a Prayer (Children's Book). The sixth, and seventh books are in the works titled The Adventures of Tike and Tunka (Children's Book) and The Invisible (5-Part Series) along with two literary collaborations. She is currently working on two additional collaborations.

With the plethora of hats she has worn and currently wear, the moniker that stands out the most is The TV Talk Show Queen! The name was coined after she took the talk show world by storm with her show *Just So You Know Moment* with a #Twist TV Talk Show. She never planned on her TV career ending with the one show so she took it to the next level. Dr. LaShonda M. Jackson-Dean is now the owner and producer of JDI Multi-Media Network. Always looking for ways to share her servant-leadership style, she created her network with others in mind. Her network provides a platform for creating media opportunities for aspiring producers. The JDI Multi-Media Network offers something that most networks fail to consider – creative independence. The network has exclusive genres with the air of open-mic ability. The JDI Multi-Media Network welcomes creators and producers interested in adding television as a medium for conveying their message to the world. The JDI Multi-Media Network uses mass communication to include digital streaming as well as social media platforms.

To think she almost let go, willing to throw in the towel on any and everything possible. In retrospect, her breakthrough was important not only for her but for others as well. Had she remained on the floor waddling in her tears and regret, she would have forfeited the opportunity to lead other women out of their darkness. Be willing to acknowledge that your healing may be for more than just you.

To think she allowed a traumatic experience that she had no control over to control her. This inflicted trauma tricked her into believing that she was less because of it. She punished herself for a crime she did not consent to. She had to learn to change things to what she could control or control how she respond to things she could not control.

To awake from this trying life experience, she was able to live past her trauma. She had to finally realize that there was no cavalry coming to save her. She had to decide to go on Calvary for her salvation (Mark 5:34). Through her own personal expedition, the vision for her life was restored. This restored vision caused an awakening in her that has purposed her to share with others.

To move forward, it should be understood that for everything, there is a time and a season, not always occurring in tandem. There will be incidents in our lives that cause us to shut down, teaching us that we all respond differently to trauma and things that hurt us. We should all recognize that negative experiences despite the magnitude of the trauma, can still be overcome. We can rebuild and we can live again.

For those reading this chapter of Dr. Jackson-Dean's life story and feel stagnant in their growth or recovery, she wants you to know a few things:

1) If she could push through, so can you (Phil. 4:13).
2) Take your total wellness to heart. Your mind, body and spirit are one and should be treated accordingly.
3) Be conscious of your meditation and prayer time.
4) Speak positive affirmations and biblical scriptures over your life.
5) Eliminate stress.
6) Create a proper diet and get plenty of exercise.
7) Protect your peace.
8) Last but not least, recognize your worth and live it. You deserve to be successful and the metrics for **_your_** success are subjective.

About the Author: Dr. LaShonda M. Jackson-Dean, a thought-provoking motivational speaker who gracefully assists others, in changing the trajectory of their lives.

Dr. Jackson-Dean captivates audiences with strategic methods of resilience and progression.

Whether speaking to individuals or groups, Dr. Jackson-Dean's message is always spot on and relevant for those who want to reach the next level in their lives. If you need guidance on execution and implementation for life-changing results, contact Dr. LaShonda M. Jackson-Dean for your next event.

Contact Dr. Jackson Dean on:

FB: DrLaShondaJacksonDean

IG: JDIMultiMediaNetwork

IG: DrLaShondaJacksonDean

TW: DrLJD_Author
Website: www.DrLaShondaJacksonDean.com
Website: www.JacksonDeanInvestments.com
ROKU: JDI Multi-Media Network

A LIFE NOT IMAGINED

Wendy H. Jones - Scotland

I can do all this through him who gives me strength
Phil 4:13 (NIV)

My life has certainly not played out the way I had imagined. Born into a working class, single parent-family in Dundee, Scotland, I went home to a flat or apartment, in the old tenements in Dundee, with few rooms, an outside toilet and a large extended family. I don't remember this as we moved when I was six months old to a larger airy council flat. Though money wasn't plentiful, I never went without, and I knew I was loved by my extended family. My childhood was happy, filled with laughter, sun and rain – lots and lots of rain. After all, I am Scottish, the land of four seasons in one day.

I believe the quickly changing seasons of our distinctive Scottish weather prepared me for the life ahead. It formed me, like Paul, *to be content in every circumstance (Phil 4:11)*, whether this be in my Christian faith or in life itself. I knew, from a young age, that God had his hand on my life. I was brought up Catholic and went to church every day before school. I was happy in my life, my faith and was prepared to spend my life in Scotland. However, God had other, greater and hugely wild plans for my life.

When I was fifteen, I applied to do nurse training in the Queen Alexandra's Royal Naval Nursing Service (QARNNS), and much to my amazement was accepted. This led to my leaving Scotland at the age of eighteen on a five-hundred-mile journey to England. For a wee lassie from Dundee, this trip was an adventure in itself, and scary as all get-out. My nurse training and faith went hand in hand as I prayed both for and with patients. I reached the rank of Petty Officer by the age of twenty-one, which was unheard of. Life was good and I was on top of the world. It was during this time, I met Christians from other denominations and investigated those, in order to learn more about them. I was able to talk freely about my faith with other Christians, and explore it more fully. At the same time, I was discovering more about life and other cultures, so important for the way in which my future would play out. My first tip to you: do not be afraid to explore other areas of life, even if it means stepping out of your comfort zone. Out of your comfort zone is where you learn the most.

On leaving the QARNNS I did my Ophthalmic Nursing Course at Moorfields Eye Hospital in London. That was quite random, or so I thought, as I wanted to be a children's nurse. Hold that thought. It's important. On completing the course, I joined the Queen Alexandra's Royal Army Nursing Corps on a short service commission, of three years. That turned into seventeen. The Army sent me to do my children's nurse training at Great Ormond Street Children's Hospital which led to several postings around the world including Hong Kong, Germany, Cyprus, Gibraltar and Israel. Yes. Israel. Remember what I said about that Ophthalmic course, well St

John's Ophthalmic Hospital in Jerusalem asked the Army if they could send an ophthalmic-trained children's nurse to help them improve their children's services. I was chosen from a cast of one. Jerusalem was amazing as you can imagine, working and socialising with both Palestinians and Israelis' a joy. I loved the culture, the food, learning the language, in fact, everything about the experience. I would encourage you to explore other cultures and to live abroad if you can. This opens you up to a whole new world and allows you to grow, not only as a person but in understanding and compassion.

On the plane to Jerusalem, I sat next to a Christian gentleman who said he would pray that I find a church to attend whilst there. The person who picked me up was a Christian from New Zealand, and she attended an evangelical Church of England Church in the Old City. This became my home church and my Christian faith grew daily. One day, I went forward for prayer, although unsure why. During this time, I was filled with the Holy Spirit and felt peace like I had never previously known. I instantly went from following God and having a faith, to knowing I was his child, and He was my heavenly Father. God had his hand on my life all along and knew I had to do that ophthalmic course in order to be in the right place at the right time – a place he had ordained for me since birth. This taught me that God is in control, whatever the circumstances, something which you should believe with all your heart and soul.

I left the Army after seventeen years, holding the Rank of Major and having run the Pre-registration Nurse Education Courses for the Army, Navy and Air Force. I moved into Academia and headed up Education courses to becoming the Deputy Director of a University Faculty.

You are probably wondering where my story of winning as a woman is coming in. My life seems to be one happy and joyful experience with everything going right. Up until then it was, which is what made the next part so difficult. I became seriously ill and could not even stand up without having breathing difficulties and my oxygen levels dropping to dangerously low levels. I spent four and a half months in hospital out of six. I had numerous tests and procedures and they discovered a hole in my heart. I had heart surgery and they found three holes. This was followed by complications, and I was in hospital for three weeks instead of four days. This did not cure the breathing difficulties which were ongoing, and over twenty medications a day were not helping. I was registered disabled and moved back to Dundee to be near family. This was a low time in my life. I joined a church, but was unable to participate fully. I was no longer working, but living on a small pension with some level of Government support. I no longer felt I had a purpose and wondered why God had brought me to this place. This was when I had to hold onto the verse which anchored me: *"I can do all this through him who gives me strength" (Phil 4:13 NIV)*. This is important to remember, God is not only in control during the good times, but He is even more in control in the bad times or valleys.

It did give me time to stop and take stock of my life. It gave me time to breathe mentally and spiritually, even while I was unable to breathe physically. As an avid reader, I had always wanted to write a book. A Christian friend was on Premier Christian Radio, and I phoned up to ask a question. As the show was about publishing, I asked for advice she would give to a new writer. She advised me to write and do NaNoWriMo which is National Novel Writing Month. Good advice which I intended to follow. That Sunday at church, someone came up to me and said they had a word from God for me. They then said that I was going to make a great impact in the writing world and would reach further than I could ever imagine. That was before I'd written a word or told anyone anything. I knew then, that my illness had come about because God had a completely different plan for my life. He knew what that plan was all along. Just as Jeremiah said:

Before I formed you in the womb, I knew you
Before you were born, I set you apart
(Jer 1:5 NIV)

Many Christian authors feel God called them to write only Christian books. I knew, without a doubt, I was to write secular novels, which I have done. My adult mysteries, The Detective Inspector Shona McKenzie Mysteries have done extremely well and have hit best seller status, with one winning an International award. I was approached by a publisher, who was herself a Christian, and asked if I could write a Young Adult Series. I agreed and signed a three-book contract for the Fergus and Flora Mysteries. The first book in this series was a finalist in the Woman Alive Magazine Readers Choice Award. I was approached to write a Children's picture book and signed with a Christian Publisher. This book is essentially the story of the prodigal son, yet it's written in a way, it can be read by those of any faith. It is a way of bringing my faith in gently. This has done so well. There is also a soft toy and a colouring book, and the second book will be published by Christmas. I am an international public speaker, speaking on panels and running workshops. I founded a crime-readers festival called Crime at the Castle. I am also a writing and life coach and host a podcast to support writers. Oh, and as an added bonus, I am completely healed of whatever my mystery illness was, to every consultant's surprise. My faith is part of my journey, and I talk about this at book launches and in speaking engagements. Whilst not writing specifically Christian books, I am still bringing my Christian walk into my publishing journey, just as He knew I would.

I do not say all this to boast or to say I have done well. The glory goes to God. He had His hand on my life at every single stage. I may not have known what was going on but God certainly did. I am a living testimony to the fact that God knows what He is doing. I can say the following verse is true:

For I know the plans I have for you, declares the Lord,
Plans to prosper you and not to harm you,
plans to give you a hope and a future.
(Jer 29:11 NIV)

During my dark times it would have been easy to give up. Yet, I held firm to the above verse, knowing that it was true, even if I could not see it at that time. God had a plan for my life from the very beginning, and I know that He is good in all circumstances. No matter how bad you feel your circumstances are, God is right there beside you. Never doubt that and follow His plan for your life, walking with Him every step of the way.

I would like to go back to the title of this story, *Not the Life I imagined.* Maybe not by me but imagined in all its brilliant, exhilarating, technicolour glory by my Father in Heaven. I praise and thank Him for every minute of it and for the fact, I am a strong woman of God.

About the Author:
Wendy H. Jones is a best-selling, award-winning Scottish author, President of the Scottish Association of Writers and an international public speaker, having been a keynote speaker, panelist and workshop leader at numerous conferences worldwide. She is a writing and life coach and has two books published in the Writing Matters Series. As the Webmaster for the Association of Christian Writers, she was a contributor, editor and publisher of two anthologies for the organization and developed and built their new

website. Wendy can be contacted for speaking engagements and to run workshops through her website.

Download your free Author's Toolkit at
Website: https://www.wendyhjones.com/writing-and-marketing/
Download your free novel at
Website: https://www.wendyhjones.com

Connect with Wendy on
LinkedIn: https://www.linkedin.com/in/wendy-jones-529a7016/
Facebook: https://www.facebook.com/wendyhjonesauthor/
Twitter: https://twitter.com/WendyHJones
Instagram: https://www.instagram.com/wendyhjones/

It's Not Over

Chè Starks

*"Now unto him that is able to do exceeding abundantly above all that we ask
or think, according to the power that worketh in us"*
Ephesians 3:20, KJV

Would you believe me, if I told you that God was about to blow
your mind with blessings? Would you believe me, if I told you that
greatness is within you? Could you imagine inspiring so many people
to never give up on their dreams? I admit I had a hard time believing
this for myself. I grew up struggling with anxiety and low self-
esteem. Who was I to one day lead others into their destiny? Who
was I to make a difference and to remind someone they are
somebody? Hello, my name is Che' Starks and this is my story:

Flashback
If you would have told me when I was eighteen years old that I
would one day be the CEO of a company, I would have laughed at
you. As a matter of fact, I probably would have given some choice
words, *Yeah right!* At that stage of my journey, life hadn't painted that

picture for me. I wasn't your cookie-cutter girl or what most would have been proud of. I was the rebel, *Round around the edges*, the girl with too much attitude, and the Miss-I-Wish-You-Would kind of girl. Yep! That was me; stuck beneath so many labels. I was a hoop-earring–wearing don't-mess-with-me kind of teen. Until a mentor saw me and reminded me of whom God called me to be.

I always credit much of my success to my mentor Ms. Pat. When many only saw the broken version of me, she saw a young woman who would one day lead. For that I am still grateful.

Broken Crayons Still Color

For years, I lived in shame. I never would have imagined going on to lead a company, let alone rise above life circumstances. I experienced sexual trauma at a very young age. Statistically, that alone should have been my ticket to giving up on myself and my dreams.

At the age of three, I was told not to tell. I can remember that day very vividly. The room reeked of dust and moth balls. The carpet was a rustic orange. No adults around. Just us or so I thought. What started out as an innocent play-day with an older playmate turned into what I would later internalize as my fault. I beat myself up for years for that day, or maybe I was mad because when I did tell, I was blamed. I remember confiding in someone I thought, at the time, my young heart could trust only to be met with coldness and shame. It happened again at the ages of five, six, eight and ten. I hated myself. I contemplated suicide many times. Yet, God had another plan.

As I grew older and looked in the mirror, I hated the person I saw looking back at me. I struggled with my confidence, didn't believe that I was beautiful, and often wondered what I was here for. I couldn't see that the little girl would one day be a woman destined for greatness. All I could see then was the scars of my past, the secrets I wasn't allowed to tell, and the shame that it carried.

Overcoming Fear

I held on to that anger for many years. I passed up so many opportunities because I didn't believe that I deserved to be called to the table, let alone competent enough to have a seat. I believed the lies that the enemy constantly reminded me of: *You're nobody. Who is going to want you? CEO? Yeah right! You barely passed high school,* and so on. You see, every lie has an element of truth. Those fears echoed loud, but they were not louder than God's Word: *"For God hath not given us the spirit of fear; but of power, and of love, and of a sound mind"* (2 Timothy 1:7 KJV).

As a teen and into my adulthood, I began to study God's Word. I realized the best way to beat a bully is at his own game. So, instead of rehearsing what the world said I was not, one day I got in the mirror and confessed who the Word said I am.

AFFIRMATIONS

I AM HEALED. I AM LOVED. I AM BEAUTIFUL. I AM CONFIDENT. I AM STRONG. I FORGIVE MYSELF. I AM A BLESSING. I AM HERE FOR A REASON. I CAN MAKE A DIFFERENCE. I AM NOT ALONE. MY STORY WILL CHANGE LIVES. I AM A CHANGE AGENT. I AM POWERFUL.

You see, we all carry a conquerors anointing. But it starts with our confession and speaking life, even if we have to speak life over ourselves. My circumstances wanted me to shrink under the pain of the trauma of my past. Life wanted me to give up and believe that I wouldn't be more. I know what is like to hit rock bottom and have to start completely over. I've been there. Many think *hard times* mean the party is cancelled or time to pack up and go home, but it's not so. Some of our toughest challenges in life present the greatest opportunities if we learn how to view them properly.

Having a Winning Mindset

My life began to change when my mindset changed. For years, I talked about my goals and dreams but never really did anything towards them, until one day, when I decided enough was enough. I knew what it was like to struggle. So, why not try to succeed?

In 2017, I stepped out on faith and got my LLC and created a consulting firm. I was told that I was good at helping others in business. Turns out that became a company that empowered many entrepreneurs across the globe. Taking my journey a step further, I wanted to launch something that would empower others to have their own business. So here I go again! Another leap of faith, and I got certified as a life coach and travel advisor and tourism agency owner. I ended up training new agents around the world, and the company is still growing to this day.

So what changed? My mind. I no longer was that insecure little girl that was broken from her past. I no longer was the label of a single mom, nor the anxiety from the childhood trauma, or things I went through. I became an overcomer, and so are you!

Trust the Process

No matter what you face, you are a *winner*. Hard times can't stop you. Difficulty cannot break you. You were designed to win. Life can be tough as we all experience it in some way, shape, or form. But the key is to know that you are a *winner*.

Trusting the process is not always easy, but it's so worth it. Battles come to make us strong. What you've been through is valuable and can be used to push you into your destiny. I used the experiences from my childhood abuse to tailor a message of hope. I used the pain and rejection that I experienced growing up as fuel to tell someone they matter. There is no wasted material when it comes to living your purpose and winning in life. Take everything that you've been through, and use it as your number one reason to *soar*. Forgiveness has been a major part of this change for me. But that's another story for another day. Keep winning. Greatness looks good on you.

About the Author:

Chè Starks is the Certified Travel Advisor & the CEO of Stark Raving Travel| SRT Tours. She is a devout Worship Leader, mother of a beautiful daughter, and now International Best-Selling Author! www.starkravingtravel.com

Follow on FB https://www.facebook.com/starkravingtravel

BREATHING LIFE IN YOUR BUSINESS

Barbara Beckley

When the earth quakes and its people live in turmoil, I am the one who keeps its foundation firm."
Psalm 75:3 NLT

Thy word is a lamp unto my feet, and a light unto my path.
Psalm 119:105 KJV

I have accomplished incredible things in my life as a professional keynote speaker, two-time best-seller Amazon author, purpose strategist, and social media personality. I am the founder of the Diamond Factor LLC (the business that I love most) that assists women in discovering their purpose, passion, and drive. I love it, but I did not always feel this way and never thought I would reach these milestones in my life.

If you were to ask me ten years ago, I would have told you I was a coal-piece, not the shining diamond that I represent in my brand and message, the PPD (Purpose, Passion and Drive). Within the journey of being a lump of coal and an individual becoming a diamond, is a process that shapes, cuts, and at specific high temperature forms into the diamond. You can be a diamond in your business or a particular cause that you believe in or as you work both end, at a job and having your own business. Either way, the process will begin with you going on the journey to your ideal purpose.

When you determine in your mind what you must do to move forward in your goals and dreams, you would want to stop saying, *I wish* and start saying *I will, I am reliable, I am smart, I am worthy and blessed, I am more than a conqueror, and I am royalty* through God. You must continually tell yourself this every day and add little notes to display your belief around the kitchen, bathroom, car, and every other place that you spend your time. This ensures you remind yourself who you are and why you strive to do what you want to accomplish in your business and personal life. Both go hand in hand. When I was within the ages of seven and twelve, I was described as ugly, stupid, fat, a can't-amount-to-anything, and useless, and these were just a few.

Think about this: how did everything come to be formed within this world? Was everything not created from the living Word of God, including us, human beings? You must look at who you are in God and establish your foundation in every area of your life. God's Words build you up, educate you, and move you toward His goals for you.

So, when you know what the Word says, you can determine what God is saying and what's not of God. As I was going through the shaping of a diamond, I got negative words thrown at me. And I needed to find positive words to override the negativity. The only positives were, at the time, from my teacher and my father. They both told me in different stages in my life that I was a diamond still in rough that needed to be scrubbed to shine forth. I did not understand their concept in full. I was only seven, but I knew it was something nice because I thought diamonds were so beautiful and they told me I was too. I truly realized the full import of the meaning when I grew up and decided to start my own business. I wanted to make sure I was helping others to be able to find their purpose and do not let anything discourage them or they to self-sabotage themselves.

When I decided to start the Diamond Factor LLC and to get the branding name legal, I was told, *No one would understand what you are doing, you would struggle to obtain clients, you do not have enough education to coach other people,* and *who are you to help other individuals to find their purpose?* among others.

Then, the words did hurt, and I was confused on why would this passion, this business that I conceived inside of me be like a burning drive that could not wane nor allow me let it go. I had many conversations with God to make it go. However, it was not me but He that was ordering my step towards the business. It was when I heard a soft voice from inside saying, "Remember when you were seven" that the negative words came to attack me, bringing confusion, fear and uncertainty.

How was that handled? You received confirmation that you are getting groomed at being that diamond, yet you are reminded of the journey that you were in to get to the goal and purpose: the diamond in the rough. It turned out the negative words I received were to build me to look towards the Word of God and the positive aspect. Do remember how the Living Word of God works.

Another cutting aspect in my life was in the year 1985, at the age of seventeen. I was just about to graduate from High School, only to find out my father, *my rock*, passed on. He did not die by a sickness or accident, but murder. And he was the only person that always reminded me I had value, a special gift, and purpose in me. When he left, I felt alone, I felt fear, and I was extremely scared. Have you ever felt this way before, the feeling of wanting to give up, not having a purpose or simply wanting to be left alone?

My story about my father is something I will always share anytime to make sure people know their tragedies don't have to be an obstacle, but can be the foundation for their moving forward, a stepping stone to their strength. It also comes as reminders to boost you when you are working toward your business. Something might happen to causes an *earthquake, flood or hurricane* with aim to knock down your business, goals or faith, but again do go back to what the Word of God stated, for He give peace in the midst of the storm (Matthew 8:24-27). You have to keep your peace when a client is upset, or you start to lose revenue. Maybe, your overhead is higher than your income to the point it feels like a death has happened to you. It's part of the journey to your getting molded, so you would be ready for the next level.

When my father passed, I thought I was going to give up and simply let grief take me over, but I remembered the words, yes, the words that my natural father told me, "You are smart, amazing, and would be made into that shining Diamond." It also led me to search out what my spiritual father thinks of me and that led to my speaking the right words into the business: *This too shall pass. I will increase in my finances. I am taking a faith-walk. I do not see it now, but it's working out in the spiritual realm.* You must breathe life into your business, the people working around you, and the decision you have to make every day to keep it going. Just as I mentioned above, remember how God formed the earth with word; you have to use His word on your business, goals, and dreams. Give it life and move away from the death talk from others and yourself.

The next form of journey within the diamond-shining process is to take a self-assessment. We can be our own worst enemy, whereas we are busy looking to blame the enemy. Sometimes, your enemy is the words you think about or speaks out loud. For self-assessment, ask yourself these questions: *what talent, gift, or passion do I have in me that I want others to experience in their lives? Is there something stopping me from moving to the next level in my life? Am I holding any unforgiveness towards another person? Am I looking towards another person to fill an absolute void?* When you ask these questions, deal with them. I had to deal with all these questions to make sure I was true to myself and to make sure I was covering all bases to move forward and grow within my business. I had to pull up the mirror.

Whatever challenges you face in your life, be it the death of a loved one, the end of a career, or a breakup after a long relationship, dig deep, take all that negative energy and turn it into a positive influence for others. When you focus on sharing and caring for others, you heal in the process. It took me talking about my father's death to connect with others and help me deal with the hurt and loneliness that lingered within me. I thought I was right and ready to move forward in my business but was not. The reality is, it takes a person to be vulnerable and still dare to fight through the pain than keeping it all inside. Don't let the hurt deter you from being the person you can be.

The last process in diamond's journey is to understand that whatever happens in your business, be it the goals or financial increase etc. that you are working towards, you need to know that the Word of God brings life, understanding, and peace. You will move forward as you bring this knowledge with you. It helps with your mindset and in making solid and sound decisions. The Word should be the foundation for everything you do.

About the Author:

Barbara J. Beckley is a professional keynote speaker; a two-time best-selling author, purpose strategist, and social media personality. She is the founder and CEO of the Diamond Factor LLC which empower people to understand their PPD (Purpose, Passion, and Drive), most especially for women to overcome their challenges so they can shine like a diamond in their businesses and personal lives.

FROM ADVERSITY TO ATTAINMENT

Angela Foxworth

"Count it all joy, my brothers, when you meet trials of various kinds, for you know that the testing of your faith produces steadfastness. And let steadfastness have its full effect, that you may be perfect and complete, lacking in nothing."
James 1:2-4 ESV

"I have said these things to you, that in me you may have peace. In the world you will have tribulation. But take heart; I have overcome the world."
John 16:33 ESV

My name is Angela Foxworth aka "A Fox." I am a television talk show host, a red carpet celebrity host, a two-time best-selling author and the reigning Mrs. Georgia Woman US Majesty 2020. My life sounds almost perfect, doesn't it? I have the opportunity to be on television and interview very important people. As a best-selling author, which equals an elevated status in our world, I have a voice. And as the reigning pageant queen, it is a dream to be admired by young girls and women of all ages around the world and considered a worldly beauty. It's the life that most women dream of, right?

For some women, maybe, but, what these women don't think about is how you got there. How did you become successful? They never think about the adversity or the struggles it took to attain your dream. They never think about the rejections you have faced from countless individuals. They never think about the opportunists that surround you trying to take from you before you even get started. They never think about the long hours you put in while they were sleeping. They never think about your losses. Living your dream is the most rewarding experience you can have in life. But for most of us, the road to success was a very difficult one.

My journey started in college where I was destined for glory. I had left high school on top of the world, first black to ever be voted most popular; Second black, homecoming queen; first black to ever be a key mascot (most popular social club in high school); and was headed to College to be the next Oprah Winfrey. At least, that was the plan.

Most of us have a plan mapped out for our lives. Also, for most, that plan started at a very young age. During those early years you have not lived life long enough to truly assess what's ahead. So, you excel in your dreams because you don't operate with barriers. You may not have had many catastrophes to deal with.

But like anything else in life, sometimes, our plans can get derailed. I went on to college and after two years, got pregnant. Things did not work out with my son's father, and I had to drop out of college, *dream deferred*. I jumped right into the workforce as I was now a single, black, mother of one. I went from being a dream seeker to a statistic. I was very happy to be a mom and for three years, it was just my son and me. Then I decided to move to Atlanta, Georgia. I was told that there were so many opportunities for single black women in Atlanta that I would never find at home. So I decided to give it a try. I moved to Atlanta and shortly thereafter, I met my husband and had my second child, my daughter, *dream diminishing*. I became a housewife and mom and worked in corporate America, *dream nonexistent*. Like that, twenty years of my life passed by. I can't even recall what I did during that time. I just know that things were not good. My marriage was in trouble. My kids were in trouble. And I had been laid off from corporate America and could never seem to get back on track financially.

Adversity can be very difficult in life. Challenges will arise, plans will get derailed, and dreams can definitely be put on hold. Even more disappointing, they can become obsolete. The even sadder part is how you process your dream during a tragedy. Sometimes, we can convince ourselves that it was a pipe dream, a non-realistic expectation for our lives. Our mindset is funny that way. Often times, we process negativity in a way that makes us feel like our lives are over. So we give up, and go back to living a status quo existence.

After getting confirmation from God, I moved to another town. Like Abraham, I moved my family to an unfamiliar place. The analogy would be from the city to the country. I knew I needed a change, and I had prayed about it. By then I had reached forty and even with this move nothing had changed. Then I had a breakdown. But, with that particular break down I also had a vision of a better life for myself. What I realized at that particular time in my life was that God was re-instilling the hope that had previously been diminished.

In the midst of difficulty we have to seek God first. Sometimes we are positioned to receive hardships in our life in order for us to clearly get to our purpose. God will affirm what He truly wants from us. This is supported by the prayer: "Let thy will be done on earth as it is in heaven." You have to ask Him to provide you with a road map to your purpose. You also have to decide to believe in that vision. Begin to think about what it is you really want to do with your life. Faith without works is dead. You have to take action in order for the answered prayers to be manifested.

I began researching to find out how I could accomplish what it was I set out to do with my life, *dream re-surfacing*. Once you realize what you're purposed in your heart to do, you find the information that shows you what you need to do to achieve your dream. I began to look for opportunities that would lead me in the direction I needed to go in. Never, in my wildest dreams, did I ever think it would get me to the place I am today.

If you want something badly enough you will do whatever it takes to achieve it. This is so important. It is what separates the haves from the have-nots. It is imperative you find out every possible thing you can about what it is you need to do. How to get started. What to do once you've gotten started. What education you need? How much money will it take to start? What free resources are out there? Research is the key to success. You can't fulfill a vision if you do not have the roadmap to get to achieve it. I began to create a schedule for myself to work on the things I needed to do to fulfill this dream. So my message is very simple: *never ever give up on a dream*. Life may throw monkey wrenches at you and even boulders sometimes, but you are already equipped and have more than enough strength to keep going.

Preparation is the key to your destiny. Is it going to be easy? No, of course not. There may be times when things may seem to flow, and you're on a path of elevation. There will be other times when you hit a roadblock or a snag in the road, and you have to re-navigate in order to get back to your original destination. Do not fear this. In time, you will begin to see the patterns in your life, and use them as tools to overcome and be more determined to hit your goal each and every time. Be patient. Sometimes, we are so inundated with a microwave mentality that we cannot sit back and patiently wait for our dreams to manifest.

Remember, I'm going to say it again, faith without works is dead! If COVID-19 has not taught me anything else, it is to use the time and resting period God has allowed us to have, wisely. There have been a lot of losses with this pandemic. I have been personally affected. But, for some of us, we can either look at it as a crutch to never move forward or a catalyst to spring forward in our purpose. You see, before COVID-19, a lot of us were like the hamster on the running wheel. We would run, run, run and go, go, go and never take the time to rest. Though for some of us, it was not because we did not want to rest, but because of all the responsibilities we have, to feed our families and carry out our everyday lives duties. Most of us are not even financially secure. So look at COVID-19 as an opportunity to get off the spinning wheel to rest. When you are able to rest your mind, you will be able to think clearer and see the direction you're going a lot better. That cheese you're trying to attain on that running wheel will only be reachable, if you stop and come up with a game plan on how you can achieve your goals. As long as you are still alive and able to breathe on this earth, you have the ability to do exactly what it is you want to do. So make wise use of your time. Find mentors and people who don't mind giving you sound advice in your field. Create a support system of people who encourage and push you. Remember you are never alone in this *journey of a dreamer*, and the end result will always be major success and profit for you. Your dream will make room for your wealth. When you are doing what you are destined to do, money is going to follow. Research monetization processes and resources. Make realistic money-making goals and eventually you will begin to build your wealth. Celebrate every win in your life. If you reached a goal, no matter how big or small, you deserve to acknowledge that. The end result should be, *dream realized*. That's how you overcome adversity and get to attainment!

About the Author:

Angela Foxworth is a tv talk show host and two-time bestselling author. As a tv talk show host Angela believes in "Promoting positive reinforcement and true change in the community through the purest form of communication there is." The Angela Foxworth premieres on the Xperienc On Demand television network. And as a two-time bestselling co-author of "Pray, Slay and Collect" and author of "The Pain Behind the Smile", Angela focuses on empowering women of all ages to pursue their dreams and achieve success no matter what life challenges them with. She has will always be purpose driven. "Life with A Fox is living outside the box" and she is "always interviewing with a purpose. She will always be an advocate for fulfilling your destiny. She is married to her husband of 23 years along with her two children and first-born grandson. She currently resides in Marietta, Ga.

Stay Connected
Visit: www.theafoxshow.com
Email: afox2440@yahoo.com
IG @afoxradio

A MOTHER'S CHOICE

Davida Bilal

"I can do all this through him who gives me strength."
Philippians 4:13

Queenie dreamed of a life where she was the CEO of a corporation. There were no children, and she spent her days traveling the world to shop. She never imagined being a mother of one, let alone three before her thirtieth birthday. Her refrigerator is covered in tiny art, the sink is full of dishes, and little girl giggles echo from every room in the house. Rather than making business deals, her days are full of negotiating about snacks. Isn't it funny how things don't always go according to plan? When the kids happened, there was an added pressure that fueled her to want more than she had. Those unfulfilled wants had her depressed, isolated, and oftentimes, pissed off. Queenie had a plan for her life, but God had a better one.

Sitting at a small wooden desk, the seat hard and cold beneath her, Queenie sat staring up at her 4th-grade teacher as she announced to the class: "Open your history books and turn to chapter seven." The teacher continued, "Today's reading is about the Renaissance period." Queenie opened her book and quickly swiped through the pages until she found chapter seven. "The renaissance was a fervent period of European cultural, artistic, political, and economic 'rebirth' following the Middle Ages" (Renaissance period, 2020). As Queenie sat in awe of the first few images of the *Mona Lisa* by Leonardo Da Vinci and *David* by Michaelangelo, she felt goosebumps. They were beautiful and grand to her. She remembers the feeling was like a lifestyle of wealth and abundance.

Queenie carried those images and the feeling she had back then with her through every stage of her life. She looks at her daughters daily and sees the rebirth of herself in them, a gesture, which always leaves her filled with gratitude and realization that she too is making history. *Her story* bestowed upon her daughters will be full of wealth and abundance as she saw it in the textbook so many moons ago. Queenie's identity as a renaissance Mom is cloaked in an ever-changing and always learning passion for success. Queenie will, at all cost, give her daughters what she never had herself – choices.

Queenie was always told she acted like somebody's momma, and rightfully so. Growing up with her young cousin, it was natural for her. She always looked after and bugged her little cousin about keeping himself and the house together. In hindsight, maybe she did act like his mom. She had never known where the instinct to act like a momma came from, in part because she didn't grow up with her biological mother. Her grandmother, who the family called Betty, was the only representation of a mother she had. Betty was stoic, forward, smart, honest, and most importantly, strong. Queenie believes that she would not be who she is today if it was not for her grandmother's ability to take on the role of a mother. Thus, Queenie is in part who she is today because of her grandmother. She is strong and honest, thanks to Betty. This helps because as a child, she never thought being an adult had so many layers. Living in a non-traditional home weighed on Queenie heavily. It was not until she became pregnant with her own child that she realized that so much of how she grew up affected her.

Queenie laid in an air mattress, six months pregnant, contemplating how she had gotten to this place in life. Struggling to pull herself into her steel-toe boots and out into cold Virginian air, while carrying an extra twenty-five pound of baby, the scripture, Philippines chapter four verse thirteen, was the only strength that got her going. As she walked the three miles to the shipping yard, there were plenty of quiet moments to think. Thoughts of reflection and transformation flooded her mind. Queenie made the mature decision to become resilient and to make a conscious effort to learn from her mistakes. She envisioned a future for her unborn child and she knew it would only come to fruition if she changed her life, family, and finances. She has experienced death, loss of relationships, financial instability, and homelessness, even as she is experiencing clarity, spiritual focus, birth, and community. After years of feeling out of place in her family and not enough for the world, she finally made up her mind in her late twenties to find a way to cope.

Queenie grew up with an Islamic influence from her grandmother and adopted Christianity through a relationship she was in as a teenager. She initially thought that her desire to understand Christianity would die as the teenage relationship did, but it was not so. She found, through the reading of the Bible, that Christ gave us the freedom to choose and that Genesis 5:1 (Amplified Bible) stated that *"When God created man, he made him in the likeness of God [not physical, but in spiritual personality and moral likeness]."* Queenie realized she had a choice when she was with a child to either be happy with the life that was given or be bitter about a situation that she could not control.

Queenie's transformation from a child to a woman challenged her to eliminate the things of her life that were not a reflection of God's plan. She had a unique perspective on the impact that drugs can have on a family, being raised by a substance-abuse counselor while being the daughter of a substance abuser. Her grandmother said to her once, "You don't have to believe in Allah as long as you believe in something higher than yourself." Queenie used that as her basis to accept Christianity as her faith. So she spent time reading her Bible and making those promises to God as part of her everyday life. When God promised to never leave nor forsake us, she felt a sense of family. She felt like there was someone out there that truly gets her and accepts her. Queenie made a deliberate choice to read the Bible daily no matter what. When she was homeless, she read just as much as she did when she was sleeping on a friend's floor or living in a hotel, yet she was still being bogged down every day and every hour. She remembers walking miles from school reciting *Philippians 4:13* with every three steps hoping to God nobody tried anything, the scripture giving her a sense of protection that was supernatural. It made her walk slowly and cry on some nights while on others it made her walk fast and bold.

Now, she sees they were all hard decisions and that though she misunderstood most of them, she got through them. The more she read the Bible, the more self-aware she became. She saw everything clearer and was a lot more conscious, even about the little everyday things. It was only through her lessons and trials that she realized, in retrospect, that many things she prayed away and the things she prayed to be released from, or asked for, just started to happen. She has become empowered in knowing that she can do all things through Christ who strengthens her (Phil 4:13). So, she can say to you: *Do not strive to be perfect. Just do your best and let your heart and actions speak for you.*

Most days, you may struggle and it will be hard, however, what will be harder are the days after you make the wrong choice. Queenie has slipped on her face many times, and each time, she picked herself up and became much more intentional about her prayers and actions. She learned to pace herself, surround herself with good people, and make time for the things she wants to do. She made a promise to be the best version of herself, not just for herself but for her children.

Queenie's understanding of life was once clouded with past instability, but not anymore. She thought like many people that she could control the ultimate plan of life. She came to the realization, after her third child, that God already had a plan for her life. She changed everything, her attitude, demeanor, and words, to align herself with all that was written in the Bible. Queenie is now described as a resilient mom of three beautiful girls, and the daughter of the Almighty King. She can only teach her daughters to thrive and be just as resilient as she is. Taking the different elements of complexity her life came up with, Queenie turns her energy into an appreciation for the women before her that made the ultimate decision, to sacrifice and share their lives, which contributed to her rebirth.

So, during the cloudy days ahead, remember that we all have a choice just like Queenie did, as her grandmother did, and like your children will. I just pray a spiritual focus and deliberate plan get you through as well.

About the Author:

Self-proclaimed "Renaissance Mom," Davida Bilal wears many hats: daughter, mother, student, and entrepreneur. With an intense appetite for learning and leadership, Davida has a background in health administration, yet has a passion for real estate, finance, and building generational wealth for her family. As a mother of three beautiful, lively girls, Davida spends much of her time pouring wisdom into her itty bitty future renaissance girls.

Social Media Handles:

FB: @davidabilal
IG: @davidabilal

THE PLACES YOU WILL GO WITHOUT ALL THE WAITING

Malva Gasowski

Romans 15:4 ESV "For whatever was written in former days was written for our instruction, that through endurance and through the encouragement of the Scriptures we might have hope."

Psalm 118:24 ESV "This is the day that the Lord has made; let us rejoice and be glad in it"

"The inner drive that you have, to bring change into your life, can be lulled to sleep by the comfort of your surroundings" - Malva Gasowski

Whenever I read success stories, I thought they somehow often start from a turning point – that one moment in time that successful people refer to as a wake-up call or the starting point of their career or life change. Though it is true for them, it never happened to me. The thought fascinated me, how was I different? Does that mean I cannot be successful? As a young woman, I wondered where my moment was, when will it come, did I forget to notice it, or am I still waiting for it to appear?

Sitting on the sofa with my small children, I will hold a pile of books on my lap and enter the world of written imagination. I love reading. The stories that create in my head, once the words are read, live a life of their own. They inspire me to think outside the box, to see how I can use the circumstances that others encountered to my benefit. You do not have to experience something to take advantage of the lessons learned. But you do have to put in the effort to implement those lessons. For Romans 15:4 (ESV) says, *"For whatever was written in former days was written for our instruction, that through endurance and through the encouragement of the Scriptures we might have hope."*

Installing that love for reading into my children was an effort filled with pleasurable moments. Funny stories, and phrases or quotes from books, we would use them on different occasions, either to make us laugh, help to bypass an obstacle, or learn a life lesson.

Snuggled up on either side of me, my two youngest children sat, filled with excitement as it was book time before bed:

"Mommy, how many books can we each choose?"
"Four"
"Hurray"

They choose a specific number of books each, depending on the promptness of their process to prepare for bed.

"Oh, the places you will go" By Dr. Seuss was their first choice, a story about the ups and downs of life, the glorious moments of success, and times when you find yourself in a slump. Worst of all, the waiting place, a place where people are just waiting.

I love that story. It always ends too quickly for me. Then, we were on to the second book chosen by my daughter,
"Mommy, now my book"
And so I began to read *Waiting Is Not Easy!* By Mo Willems.
Then it hit me. Here I was cuddling before bedtime, reading to my children, stories that will ingrain values for the future. Was I living by those values? I was waiting for that one moment to call my pivotal point, but it didn't come. At almost forty years of age, I still couldn't pinpoint when THAT moment was that I announced as the changing point in my life.

I smile recalling that thought. Not because I had not achieved anything before it, but because I had achieved success by that time, and yet I was still waiting. I was a wife, a mom of three, a successful entrepreneur, running two businesses, homeschooling my children, traveling internationally, and doing multiple volunteer jobs to give back to society. Looked up to by many, an example of managing the work-life balance by others, and deemed a ball of energy by a few, who couldn't grasp how I fit so many activities in a day with three children by my side. Yet, I was still mentally waiting for that special moment, however, my actions and results were speaking different stories.

Not everyone's path has to be written into the same frame. There is no logical reason to wait for something to happen to change your life around. The comfort of saying, "I have to wait for the pivotal point before I put in the hard work" will lull you to sleep and you won't achieve your success. Your daily comfort and stability might stop you from achieving more, as you wrongly believe that there must be a big breaking point for you to be able to achieve anything substantial. It is not the turning point that matters, but the conscious, confident decision of a strong woman to take the first step in her journey to achieve success. Waiting for the pivotal moment might catch you in a trap of being concentrated on surviving and anticipating, instead of taking the reins and deciding where you want this journey of life to take you to and with whom.

It's the everyday decisions you make, from the moment you wake up to the last moment before you fall asleep. It's the steps that you take, the people that you meet and influence, and the kindness that you emanate that will bring you joy and success, no matter how big or how small it may seem to others.

Success is the nighttime cuddle of tiny loving arms, when you know you have created a safe and comfortable home for your children to flourish and grow in. Success is the laughter that you share with your significant other knowing your plans did not work out as anticipated, and still go on holding each other's hand and moving forward with love. It is achieving a momentous milestone with your team at work, where you acknowledge all the hard teamwork dedicated to the process, and you are all proud to be working together. It is being able to manage conflict in business, so it does not escalate, but gets resolved and is transformed into a learning opportunity for all involved. And it is being woken up by birds chirping in the morning while the wind sings a morning song.

No matter how big, or how small. I have learned to cherish those moments. I encourage you to do the same because *"This is the day that the Lord has made; let us rejoice and be glad in it" (Psalm 118:24 ESV)*.

When working with my clients, the first coaching session is critical. It emphasizes what is? and ends with: when will you know you have achieved success and why is it important to you? These three questions open the doors to understanding the current situation you are in, where you want to be, and what is your driving force.

What is? This is a simple question that when asked over and over again to match the description of one's life, focuses our eyes on the reality we have found ourselves in. It anchors the critical points of interest. It highlights what we ought to be grateful for. Furthermore, it brings to light, exactly what it is that we would like to change. Change is a process that happens, if we like it or not. Change is the consequence of a decision, even if your decision is to not make one. I encourage people to evaluate their 'What is?' giving them the power to single out what exactly they want to invest their time in: changing, improving, fixing, altering, or implementing. Fast forward to the second part of the coaching session, where we focus on the result of this project we have decided to concentrate on.

When will you know you achieved success? It is a question that seems rational, but extremely hard to answer. My clients have difficulty in pinpointing what it is that would make them happy, successful, or fulfilled in their lives. Just like advertisements sell experience rather than products, is the same way people, especially women, want to achieve the feeling and not specific goals. *I want to be fit. I want to be famous. I want to be an amazing mom. I want to be an understanding wife. And I want to be rich.* If you look at the makeup of these sentences they do not give you anything specific. What does "fit" mean? To some, it is a six-pack lasting eleven months out of the whole year, to others, it is being healthy with low cholesterol levels, and to me personally, it can mean fitting into specific size jeans and feeling comfortable.

The same applies to wanting to be rich. For a few it can mean having a calm life, on a farm and not worrying about bills; to others, it may mean having a happy and healthy family; to a different group of people, it may be equivalent to purchasing private jets, celebrity status or ice-cube size diamonds on their hand.

Having a mind-set of setting measurable goals, based on facts and not emotions, will make them a purpose to reach. Having a mindset of setting measurable goals, based on facts and not emotions, will transform the dreams into a purpose and an aim to reach.

The final question: **Why is this goal important to you?** Digging deep into your feelings, you can see if you are chasing an experience, an illusion, or someone else's dream. Or have you thought through why it is that you want to put in the work to achieve this goal?

All the answers to these questions will keep you accountable to yourself as you will have the intrinsic motivating factor driving you to move forward when times get tough. And they will. Birds chirping, children laughing in the garden, husband sitting by my side, while I am writing a chapter hoping to inspire others to stop a while and think about their wins, is my "What is?" This perfect moment of finding the balance I need to feel safe, loved, welcomed, and needed.

What is it that I want to achieve? I want to reach a million children and change their lives for the better. I would love to assist their parents in creating a loving home, where laughs and giggles are a norm instead of yelling and anger; where feeling safe and welcome is a given; parents giving a thousand kisses a day to their newborns; toddlers getting a thousand cuddles and kisses especially when they need love, at times asking for it in a quiet unloving way; a thousand hugs with your teen, when they run to you to share their victories; a thousand moments worth connecting with your young adult, through conversation, and genuine interest in their world; and all the way, to having a thousand reasons to call home as adults, not because they need to but because they want to.

I want to change the lives of a million children by helping their parents implement positive parenting. When will I know I have achieved success? When I get half a million clients comment or share feedback with me, that my work has helped individual families.

Why is this important to me? Because having children of my own I see how they blossom. How much love and moments of connection they need. How amazing it is to be able to give them the emotional closeness and experience of positive parenting, to give them a voice and equip them with resilience and problem-solving skills. And seeing the influence my children have on their friends implementing the same strategies present in our home. This is a personal experience backed up by years of education and endless hours helping others thrive that will change the dynamic of individual families, but might have a ripple effect on the future of this generation of kids. Is it a big goal? Yes, it is. Is it possible? I sure hope so, for the benefit of the children and their close, long-lasting positive relationship with their parents.

Remember that one advertisement of baby products, that made you stop channel hopping? That cute little baby, so innocent and sweet, breastfed by its mother, rested and relaxed. The baby would later smile at the father, who was beaming with pride. This image might bring you back to that one photo you adore of yourself as a baby, or your own babies, where, if you close your eyes, you will still be able to smell that sweet intoxicating aroma of a newborn's head, that you could not help but give a million kisses to in a day. This advertisement might evoke a range of positive emotions, a smile, or a giggle, as they take you back to one amazing experience filled with pure joy. I wish you all to have these amazing memories present daily as stepping stones in building your personal and professional life.

About the Author:

Malva Gasowski is an international business trainer, coach, and speaker for corporate soft hr skills. She is also a parenting coach and couples counsellor working with parents and couples from all walks of life, implementing the positive parenting approach to building closeness in the family.

She helps women become happy moms, with a positive home and balanced work-life. She helps dads be fulfilled in their parenting roles as well as helping them manage their team at work. She helps couples find their spark and resolve their issues to build a passionate and loving partnership. She helps single people grow a loving relationship with theselves to feel fulfilled in their life.

As an international business trainer and coach, she helps people achieve success in their companies (top international corporations). She has conducted training sessions, speeches and coaching sessions, among others, in talent management, communication, negotiation, people management, motivation and evaluation of employees, techniques of preparing and conducting presentations, self-presentation, mindfulness and well-being, stress management, training in critical and analytical thinking, conflict resolution and cooperation in business, training, beauty, services and production sectors of the industry.

She is the creator of *Coaching - Mother and all*, supporting parents in their parenting journey.

Malva's passion is to make the world a better place through communication and creating a successful business while being a fulfilled parent and happy couple.

You can connect with Malva at:
Access your complimentary coaching session with Malva referring to "Women Win: Against All Odds"
Email: malva@coaching-mother-and-all.com
https://www.coaching-mother-and-all.com/
www.facebook.com/coaching.mother.and.all
www.instagram.com/coaching.mother.and.all
Positive Relationship Support Group
https://www.facebook.com/groups/231334044891054/

After hundreds of applications and submissions, Jesus, Coffee, and Prayer Christian Publishing House LLC.
Is Proud to Announce our 1st Influential Women Who Win Honorees!

The women that you will meet on the next few pages are bold, smart, innovative, and making major moves in their Speaker, Author, &/or #Girlboss business!
Glean, Grow, & Glow from our Inaugural Influential Women Who Win.
Get Connected with these Global Leaders Today!

Interested in More Speaker, Author, or #Girlboss business Opportunities, Resources, & Connections?
Join our FREE Group Today!
https://www.facebook.com/groups/speakerauthorgirlbosses

Jesus, Coffee, and Prayer Presents: Influential Women Who Win (IWWW)

Tina Ramsay

CEO: Multifarious & Company, LLC (Heal The Honeypot)
Camden, SC

"I know that I can do anything that I put my mind too, but it doesn't mean that I should do everything. I do what I love, and I am willing to grow, be teachable and adjust as needed along the way. I am brave enough to be myself even when there isn't a place for me in the room, I'm bold enough to create my own space to win."

About the IWWW:
Tina Ramsay is a Certified Female Wellness/Empowerment Coach, Menstrual Health Advocate, Author, Public Speaker, Community Volunteer, Wife, Mother, and the Founder/CEO of HealTheHoneypot.com. Her Mission is to educate women and teens on the importance of healing the mind, body, and honeypots

naturally. She has Fun Engaging Healthy Conversations about topics that affect all-females in the hopes of helping women make better life and health decisions.

Connect with this Queen:

HealTheHoneypot.com (Tina.JewelPads.com)

https://www.facebook.com/healthehoneypot

https://instagram.com/heal_the_honeypot

Janee Culpeper

CEO: Financial Healing For Women
Oklahoma City, OK

"I am winning in this season by getting in alignment with the assignment God sent me to accomplish. He is teaching me to prepare financially, emotionally and mentally for the work that is ahead to help women heal their finances and win in their life! "

About the IWWW:

Janee Culpeper was born and raised in Los Angeles, California, although she currently resides in Oklahoma City. She is a graduate of Langston University, where she pursued a Bachelor's degree in Business Management and continued her education with a Masters of Business Leadership from Mid-America Christian University. She also has been through a degree of life-altering experiences, trials, and a series of financial failures. As a result of her experiences birthed "Financial Healing for Women," an organization geared towards helping individuals take charge of their financial lives through teaching biblical principles partnered with tangible techniques! Janee loves to see women all over the world become finally free, free from the bondage of debt, lack of financial education, generation hindrances. Her goal to help women live the abundant life God says they can live! Janee hosts financial sessions throughout the Oklahoma City areas and also provides coaching sessions for women just like you!

Connect with this Queen:
https://www.financialhealingforwomen.com
https://www.facebook.com/FinancialHealingForWomen/
https://www.instagram.com/financialhealingforwomen/

Tamika L. Blythers

CEO: Eduvizon LLC
Columbus, GA

"3 things attributing to me winning in this season are: Focusing on who I am, valuing what I bring to the table, and mastering my craft & talents."

About the IWWW:

T.L. Blythers is a best-selling author, dynamic educator, consultant, entrepreneur, master trainer/facilitator & transformational speaker. Her business, Eduvizon LLC provides empowerment education and hosting/emcee services designed to enhance, provide clarity, transform & achieve desired premium results. T.L. Blythers stands firmly on the life principle, "You are a product of your expectations, not the limitations."

Connect with this Queen:
www.iamtlblythers.com
https://www.facebook.com/tl.author
http://instagram.com/tlblythersauthor

Jana Johnson

CEO: Bellanaj Cosmetics LLC
Norfolk, VA

"I win in this season despite a worldwide pandemic because, God allowed me to launch a successful business. I win because I did this to help other women find their beauty and realize that nothing is impossible. If you have a vision, a plan, and an ear to hear, then the sky's the limit."

About the IWWW:
Jana Johnson is a curvy plus size model, mogul and entrepreneur. Her career in the beauty industry spans more than 20+ years. She is a single mother of 2 boys.

Connect with this Queen::
www.bellanajcosmetics.llc
The Branded Called J (Facebook)
@bellanajcosmeticsllc (IG)

Sophie Zollmann

CEO: SophieZo, LLC
Nashville, TN

"I am winning in this season by continuing to work with my coach and his team, saying yes to courses, workshops and other opportunities that will help me grow my business, and expanding my team as often as needed to make sure I can do what is needed to win and not be bogged down in the day-to-day minutiae of the business and life."

About the IWWW:
Sophie Zollmann, is the secret weapon behind many small businesses. Being someone's right-hand support system is where her genius lies. And SHE LOVES to get stuff done! She is a Certified Online Business Manager, Certified Social Media Manager, and Certified Customer Acquisition Specialist. She is also a member of the International Association of Online Business Managers.

Connect with this Queen:
https://sophiezo.com/
https://facebook.com/sophiezo/
https://instagram.com/thesophiezo/

Love Scott

CEO: Aura of Amouri
Los Angeles, CA

"Every level is a greater test to become the best version of yourself.
"

About the IWWW:
Lovey Scott is a 34-year-old disabled woman who suffered from a mini stroke and fell off a cliff while hiking. She uses her story to inspire others and prove there is still light at the end of the tunnel.

Connect with this Queen:
Follow on social media:
Facebook- Aura of Amouri
Ig @Amouriscott

Evoni Seigler

CEO: Eafbeauty

St. Augustine, Florida

"There can be a million sellers but there is only one you. Use yourself to your full advantage."

About the IWWW:

Evoni is a passionate and creative master wig maker who has continued to conquer her fears of new opportunities and has created a brand to empower women. She is extremely comfortable with her femininity. She is continuously perfecting her platform to create a safe space for women to bask in theirs.

Connect with this Queen:
www.eafbeauty.com
www.facebook.com/eafbeauty
www.instagram.com/eafbeauty

Cynthia Washington

CEO/Authorpreneur: The Novel Daisy Venus
Bedford, TX

"I want to inspire people who I meet and let them know that it's never too late to live out your dreams. You can overcome any obstacles in your life."

About the IWWW:

Cynthia D. Washington is a proud mother of 3 adult sons. Edward, Jose and Desmond. She is the middle child of 8 children. 4 girls and 4 boys. Raised by her single mom. Cynthia has always enjoyed writing poetry reading and expressing her thoughts. So becoming an author is a dream come true. Cynthia grew up in East Texas and now resides in Dallas TX with her family. She is busy planning her next novel.

Connect with this Queen:
Follow on FB:
The Novel Daisy Venus

Pauline Atkinson

CEO/Authorpreneur
Wheatley Heights, New York

"A tip on how to win this season is to Believe in yourself. Pray and Meditate for what is desired. Receive and Achieve the blessing to your fullest potential. You are Worthy!"

About the IWWW:

Queen P is the Author of "When The Mood Is Right A Poetry Journey ". Her desire is to motivate, inspire and uplift people through poetry writing. Queen P resides with her loving family in Long Island, New York .

Connect with this Queen:
Website: www.Queenppoetry.com
FB Business: Queen P
IG Business: @queenppoetry123

Tamala Coleman

CEO: NSpire Christian Magazine, Inc. & TC Praise Productions, LLC

Powder Springs, GA

"You may experience many obstacles in life. Yet you must keep moving forward and don't stop trying to achieve your God given dream. You will win if you faint not."

About the IWWW:

Tamala Jenise Coleman is a Best Seller Author, Podcast Radio Host, Director and Producer and Minister for Christ who strives to empower women and everyone she meets with her Faith.

Connect with this Queen:

Website: www.nspirechristianmagazine.com
Facebook: https://www.facebook.com/NSpire-Christian-Magazine-103895321318465/?modal=admin_todo_tour
Instagram: https://www.instagram.com/iam_tamalacoleman/

Krystal Vernee'

CEO: Simply SHE
Fort Washington, MD

"I win because I am a black woman and I am empowered. Because I am empowered, I can empower others. I will empower others to define themselves so that they can apologetically be themselves and walk in their purpose. When the women that I coach walk in their purpose, they win, just like I win. "

About the IWWW:

Krystal Vernee' is a serial womenpreneur, author, speaker and women empowerment coach. She has always been passionate about serving her community and helping others. Krystal encourages others to tap into their zone of genius through the Simply SHE podcast and Slay Hard Everyday Coaching program. It is her ultimate goal to help women eliminate self-limiting beliefs, gain clarity around who they are, what they want and get results.

Connect with this Queen:
www.isimplyshe.com
www.facebook.com/isimplyshe
www.instagram.com/i_simply_she

Fharren Mason

CEO: Infinite Styles By Fharren
Dallas, Texas

"Keep praying, keep pushing and Keep God first one all things."

About the IWWW:
Fharren Mason is the CEO of Infinite Styles by Fharren. She aspires to help people find their inner confidence by discovering more about themselves, loving themselves, and even earn more income by demanding their worth through fashion.

Connect with this Queen:
Website: www.nfinitestylesbyfharren.com
FB: Infinite Styles By Fharren
IG: @infinitestylesbyfharren

Ilka Tamar

CEO: Model/Author/Speaker
Orlando, FL by way of Puerto Rico

"This season I finally did the release of my online platform modeling and confidence called MetaMorphosis Mentorship. It's One on One 12 week program designed to help students address and rediscover their inner strengths to achieve self-confidence and empowerment thru modeling skills."

About the IWWW:

Ilka Tamar is an experienced, energetic and multifaceted individual with over 20 years of experience as a model and certified modeling and confidence coach. Her main focus is using modeling as a tool for self-esteem and empowerment, allowing young girls, teens and adults to help achieve a remarkable inside-out metamorphosis with all the students she work with!

Connect with this Queen:
Website- www.ilka-tamar.com
Facebook page- Ilka Tamar
IG- metamorphosismentorship

Katrina McCain

CEO/Authorpreneur
Greensboro, NC

"I win in this season by setting tangible goals and not letting any personal excuse stop me from obtaining those goals."

About the IWWW:
Katrina is the author of a collection of poetry entitled "Because She Decided To Love" released in November 2019. Growing up in a small town of 5500 people did not stifle the big dream that brewed inside of her for years. One faithful night when she could no longer ignore God's tug on her heart to dive back into my writing, she started the journey of becoming a published author on vacation with my family.

Connect with this Queen:
www.poetkatrinamccain.com
www.facebook.com/poetkatrinamccain
www.instagram.com/poetkatrinamccain

Nakia Harrell

CEO: K Harrell's Financial Services
Charlotte, NC

"I win by powering through every day to gain more clients. I network extensively and my family helping and supporting me is very important to me."

About the IWWW:
Nakia holds her MBA and an MS in Public Accounting. She has been in accounting industry for 7+ years. She worked in "Big" banking for 13 years. She is married and has 2 boys, two stepsons, and 2 grandchildren.

Connect with this Queen:
Website: www.moneydoesgrowontreeskhfs.com
FB @KHarrellsFS
IG @kharrellsfsgetmoremoney

Ashley Little

CEO: Ashley Little Enterprises, LLC
Nashville, TN

"Submit & Surrender to God is how you WIN. Next, you have to do the WORK. Faith without works is dead and remember to stay humble and consistent. Lastly, reach back and help someone else. What you make happen for others God will make happen for you."

About the IWWW:
Ashley Little is The CEO/Founder of Ashley Little Enterprises, LLC which encompasses her Media, Consulting Work, Writing, Ghost Writing, Book Publishing, Book Coaching, Project Management, Public Relations & Marketing, and Empowerment Speaking. In addition, she is an Award-Winning Serial Entrepreneur, Editor-In-Chief of Creating Your Seat At The Table International Magazine, TV/Radio Host, Speaker, Host, Philanthropist, Business Coach, Investor and 8X Best Selling Author.

Connect with this Queen:
Website: www.ashleylittleenterprises.com
Facebook Page: Ashley Little Facebook: T.A.L.K Radio & TV Network, LLC
Instagram:_ashleyalittle @thehbcuexperiencemovement
@talkradiotvnet_

Kymberly Lowery

CEO: Wonderfully Made
Antioch, TN

"Everything happens for a reason, lasts a season, or impacts a lifetime. During this season, I have seen my business grow more than I could have imagined. Through hard work and dedication, I have been able to realize my dreams and WIN!"

About the IWWW:
Kymberly Lowery has been in the IT business for 20 years and she is still going strong! She is an IT geek and loves what she gets to do! She is a website designer, branding specialist, and business development expert. Her aim is to help women be successful in business by building a winning brand!

Connect with this Queen:
Website: kymberlylowery.com
Facebook: fb.me/wonderfullymadewebsites
IG: instagram.com/iamklowery

Sadaqa Calhoun-Redus

CEO: Asè Holistic Health (KIM'B)LLC
West Chester, Ohio

"How I win in this season: I give love, I show love and I listen. In this season that we are in people need love and they need someone to just listen so they can release."

About the IWWW:
Sadaqa has always had a love for helping people. She has the gift of healing and she is a natural light. People are drawn to her and often confide in her with their imbalances and issues.

Connect with this Queen:
Website: www.AseSadaqa.com
FB: Asè
IG: AseSadaqa

Dr. Tonya Blackmon

CEO: Conglomerate Empowerment
Las Vegas, NV

"Success is Planned! Focus & Write your Vision. Execute your Strategic Plan. Live the Life of Your Dreams!"

About the IWWW:

Dr. Tonya Blackmon, a 10-year Business Strategist, is the creator of the "CGE Journey to Millions Blueprint" signature program. Her 4 Step System help Women-owned Small businesses get Big government contracts and achieve their dreams.

Connect with this Queen:
Website:www.congempowerment.biz
https://www.facebook.com/conglomerate7/
https://www.instagram.com/drtonyab_live

Tiffany D. Bell

CEO: UnCommon Courage, LLC (CEO & Founder) &
Success Women's Conference (Co-Owner)
Gulfport, MS

"My personal philosophy on what we must do to "win" in all seasons is based around these principles. Press forward because focus always proceeds success. Refuse to let others create boundaries for you. Stay true to God's truth, purpose, and plan for your life. Serve others by adding value to their lives. "

About the IWWW:

Tiffany D. Bell is an author, speaker, and nonprofit strategist. As an executive director of a nonprofit, Tiffany has over 25 years of experience in community outreach and leadership training. She is on a mission to show young women how to step forward in their power when faced with difficult circumstances.

Connect with this Queen:
Website: www.uncommoncourage.cc
https://www.facebook.com/UnCommonCourage.cc/
https://www.instagram.com/uncommon_courage?r=nametag

Canila Gist

CEO: Your Story Matters
Winston Salem, NC

"How you win: by staying faithful to God , allowing Him to take complete control over your life. God words say 'Walk by faith not by sight.' Therefore, be determined, dedicated, and hungry for God righteousness. Birth your purpose, that you were already destined to complete!"

About the IWWW:
Meet this southern soul who is born and raised in North Carolina. Motivational Speaker/Author of " Your Story Matters." Canila Gist helps women of faith who deal with traumatic experiences: including domestic violence, verbal abuse, molestation, and much more heal through the word of God. Canila will help you rediscover your voice.

Connect with this Queen:
www.yourstorymattersonline.com

Dayna Simms-Faulk

CEO: The Upscale Legacy Group, LLC
Columbus, NJ

"As a Business Mentor and Financial Coach, my purpose is to take individuals from Dreaming About It To Living IT."

About the IWWW:
Dayna Marie is an entrepreneur, author, speaker and success strategist with career that spans over two-decades in the financial services industry. After 10 years with the New Jersey based Fortune 100 company, Dayna Marie says she "donated her job back to the economy" to solely focus on financial wellness for families nationwide. Dayna says nothing has been more rewarding than the impact her serving has had on others and seeing them win!

Connect with this Queen:
Website:www.iamdaynamarie.com
facebook:
https://www.facebook.com/TheCreditFixChic/posts/411934436030159
Instagram: www.instagram.com/iamdaynamarie.com

Angela Parker

CEO: ANGELS TAX SERVICES LLC
Chicago, IL

"I keep God first in my life, I take a negative situation and turn it into a positive. I treat people the way I want to be treated no matter what the situation may appear to be."

About the IWWW:
Angels Tax Services LLC believe in Complete and Reliable service.

Connect with this Queen:
Website: www.angelstaxservicesllc.com
Facebook: https://www.facebook.com/angelstaxservicesllc
Instagram: https://www.instagram.com/angelstaxservices/

Mala Kennedy

CEO: Mala Kennedy Founder/Coach/Writer
Margaret River, Western Australia

"Make tiny commitments to yourself and build on them. Consistently commit to these small, daily things, and strengthen your self-trust and intuition by showing up for yourself and also build your capacity for success."

About the IWWW:
Mala helps women shift from self-doubt to self-love so they can feel confident. She works with language, emotions and body and their relationship to the self to facilitate lasting shifts in their life so they can truly find their voice. Mala is a life coach, eft practitioner, writer, podcaster, and mama. She is on a mission to help women prioritize self-care and self-acceptance. To ensure they give themselves permission to always be their authentic self and speak their truth so they can experience joy in all areas of their lives.

Connect with this Queen:
Website: https://malakennedy.com
FB: https://www.facebook.com/malaloves
IG: https://www.instagram.com/malaloves

Adrienne Pearson

CEO/CoFounder: SACI Culture, LLC
Houston, TX

"During this season I will win by staying consistent, being persistent, and knowing when to pivot."

About the IWWW:

Adrienne is a teacher who seeks to inspire women to achieve their maximum potential in life. Inspired by the need to reach her next level in life as an empty nester, she was driven to help other women of color reach the next level in their lives. Her motto: "Each of us is on a life journey, but we aspire to take the journey collectively."

Connect with this Queen:
Website: www.saciculture.net
FB: www.facebook.com/saciculture
IG: www.instagram.com/saciculture

Milli Mills

CEO: Millhouse Entertainment
Austin, TX

"To Win in this Season, one must put his trust in God. In the Bible, there are 5,467 promises from God for us including that he will never leave us or forsake us. Thus, we must learn to rely solely on Him and rest in Him each and every day."

About the IWWW:
Milli Mills is an American Radio Talent, Published Author, and CEO/Founder of Millhouse Entertainment. She has over 25 years of broadcast/radio/tv/film experience under her belt. Milli holds a Bachelor of Arts in Theatre/Communication and a Master of Arts in Organizational Management.

Connect with this Queen:
www.millhouseentertainment.com

Ashley Marie Knight & Qiana Cannon

CEO: Words Unite Bookstore & Event Center LLP.
Austin, TX

"Women can win through partnerships and connection. My business partner and I always say, start where you are, use what you have, do what you can."

About the IWWW:

Ashley & Qiana are two best-selling authors stepping out to make a difference in their community through literature and community service. They believe that Words have the power to unite us all!

Connect with these Queens:
Website: http://words-unite-bookstore-and-event-center.square.site/
Social Media; Facebook - Words Unite Bookstore
Instagram - Words Unite Bookstore

LaTasha Gatling

CEO: Mommy Morebucks. LLC
Washington, DC

"In order to WIN in this season I've activated my Insane Faith. That means I am trusting the process and preparing for opportunity in my purpose. Working on professional development, patience and intentionality has brought me so much further than I could've imagined! Have you activated your Insane Faith?"

About the IWWW:
LaTasha Gatling, is the founder of Mommy Morebucks LLC. She is an Entrepreneurial Purpose Coach that assists entrepreneurs with strategic solutions so they can be successful at whatever they choose. With my 11 years' experience, she is able to utilize her skills and expertise to create opportunity generating experiences for her clients. She looks forward to future speaking engagements and changing the world while walking in her purpose!

Connect with this Queen:
Website:
www.mommymorebucks.com
Facebook- Mommy Morebucks
Instagram- @mommymorebucks

There is Still Room for YOU!

Queen,

If you have read this entire book, then you have been encouraged, inspired, challenged, and equipped to WIN in this season and the NEXT!

My prayer is that you are blessed beyond measure in all that you do and everything you touch~ In Jesus Name!

■■■

If You Have Read these stories but you still have doubts about your ability to BOSS UP and Win in this season; I encourage you to get to know a man named Jesus.

He is the sweetest friend, I know.

If you would like to WIN on Purpose with a Purpose, read this prayer aloud to draw nearer to the Cross. (Jesus Christ that is)

Salvation Prayer

Dear Lord Jesus, I know that I am a sinner, and I am in need of a Savior. I ask for Your forgiveness of my sins. I believe that You died on the cross for my sins and rose on the 3rd day to give me life. I turn from my sins and invite You to come into my heart and life. I want to trust and follow You as my Lord and Savior. I believe that I am a new creature in You. I recognize that I am a Winner in You. In Jesus Name I pray all these things.

Amen!

If you read that Prayer aloud and believe it to be so; then I welcome, you into the BEST Winners Circle of them All... The Family & Body of Christ!

I encourage you to find a good bible-based church or community of believers to support and encourage you to seek His face.

If you gave your life to Christ after reading this book or saying this prayer, I'd love Celebrate and hear from you!
Email us: info@jesuscoffeeandprayer.com

May God keep you until the next appointed time!

Your Sister in Christ,

Min. Nakita Davis

CEO & Founder of
Jesus Coffee and Prayer
Christian Publishing House LLC.

Made in the USA
Columbia, SC
28 September 2020

21414040R00080